Oliver Optic

Sea and shore: The tramps of a traveller

Oliver Optic

Sea and shore: The tramps of a traveller

ISBN/EAN: 9783337210724

Printed in Europe, USA, Canada, Australia, Japan

Cover: Foto ©Andreas Hilbeck / pixelio.de

More available books at www.hansebooks.com

THE UPWARD AND ONWARD SERIES.

SEA AND SHORE;

OR,

THE TRAMPS OF A TRAVELLER.

BY

OLIVER OPTIC,

AUTHOR OF "YOUNG AMERICA ABROAD," "THE ARMY AND NAVY STORIES," "THE WOODVILLE STORIES," "THE BOAT-CLUB STORIES," "THE STARRY FLAG SERIES," "THE LAKE-SHORE SERIES," ETC.

WITH THIRTEEN ILLUSTRATIONS.

BOSTON:
LEE AND SHEPARD, PUBLISHERS.
NEW YORK:
LEE, SHEPARD AND DILLINGHAM.
1872.

TO

MY YOUNG FRIEND

CHARLES HUDSON,
OF CHICAGO,

This Book

IS AFFECTIONATELY DEDICATED.

THE UPWARD AND ONWARD SERIES.

1. *Field and Forest;* OR, THE FORTUNES OF A FARMER.

2. *Plane and Plank;* OR, THE MISHAPS OF A MECHANIC.

3. *Desk and Debit;* OR, THE CATASTROPHES OF A CLERK.

4. *Cringle and Cross-Tree;* OR, THE SEA SWASHES OF A SAILOR.

5. *Bivouac and Battle;* OR, THE STRUGGLES OF A SOLDIER.

6. *Sea and Shore;* OR, THE TRAMPS OF A TRAVELLER.

PREFACE.

"SEA AND SHORE" is the sixth and last of the ONWARD AND UPWARD SERIES, in which Phil Farringford, in company with his friend Larry Grimsby, has some experience as a traveller. The story includes the cruise of the Blanche, a first-class yacht, which goes to the Bermuda Islands, across the Atlantic, up the Baltic, and along the shores of the Mediterranean. The various "tramps" of these young gentlemen are in the Bermudas, in Norway, Sweden, on the Rhine, and in other parts of Europe, though the volume is in no sense a book of travel. The only object of the writer was to tell his story, in which he has endeavored to make his heroes worthy the respect of the reader, and their life and character worthy of imitation.

The unpleasant relations between Larry Grimsby and his cousin Miles lead to a yacht race from New York to the Bermudas, and the incidents of the story are based mainly on the persistent hostility of Miles, who seeks to injure, and even destroy, his cousin. But Larry has a true Christian spirit, and in the end, when his bitter enemy is sick, "even unto death," and is deserted by his friends and dependants, seeks him out, nurses him with the tenderness of a woman, saves his life, and, what is better, redeems and reforms his character. If it was not Phil who did this, it was his influence which inspired his friend to do it.

This volume closes the series, and leaves Phil comfortably settled, and still pursuing his Onward and Upward career. We are sorry to leave him, for we always prefer old friends to new acquaintances. We hope the venerable judge on the shores of the Pacific is not the only one who shares this regret with us, and we indulge our own vanity in quoting a few lines from his kind letter: "Do you know, I like your Phil Farringford ever so much, and shall be sorry to bid him good by, for he is a noble fellow and a fine character. Therefore I hope his successor will not disgrace him, but will do full justice to his predecessor."

HARRISON SQUARE, BOSTON.
April 20, 1870.

CONTENTS.

CHAPTER I.
PAGE
IN WHICH PHIL AND LARRY TALK OVER THINGS PAST, PRESENT, AND TO COME. 11

CHAPTER II.
IN WHICH PHIL AND LARRY GO ON BOARD OF THE BLANCHE. 25

CHAPTER III.
IN WHICH PHIL ENGAGES A SECOND MATE FOR THE BLANCHE. 39

CHAPTER IV.
IN WHICH LARRY VISITS THE WHITEWING, AND PHIL GETS THE BLANCHE UNDER WAY. 53

CHAPTER V
IN WHICH PHIL DISCOVERS THAT THE WHITEWING GAINS ON THE BLANCHE. 67

CHAPTER VI.
IN WHICH PHIL SPEAKS VERY CANDIDLY TO THE SECOND MATE. 80

CHAPTER VII.
IN WHICH PHIL DISPOSES OF THE SECOND MATE. . . . 94

CHAPTER VIII.
IN WHICH PHIL BOARDS THE WRECK OF THE WHITE-WING. 108

CHAPTER IX.
IN WHICH PHIL TAKES MILES GRIMSBY AND OTHERS ON BOARD THE BLANCHE. 122

CHAPTER X.
IN WHICH PHIL RELIEVES THE HERMIA, AND LISTENS TO LARRY'S STORY. 136

CHAPTER XI.
IN WHICH PHIL AND LARRY MAKE SOME NEW ACQUAINTANCES AT ST. GEORGE. 150

CHAPTER XII.
IN WHICH PHIL AND LARRY DINE AT THE GOVERNOR'S, AND A QUARREL ENSUES. 165

CHAPTER XIII.
IN WHICH PHIL AND LARRY DECLINE VARIOUS OFFERS. . 179

CHAPTER XIV.
IN WHICH PHIL AND LARRY TAKE ANOTHER TRAMP, AND AN AFFAIR OF HONOR IMPENDS. 194

CHAPTER XV.
IN WHICH PHIL AND LARRY WITNESS THE CAPTURE OF A MAN-EATER. 208

CHAPTER XVI.
IN WHICH PHIL AND OTHERS ARE CONFOUNDED BY A MYSTERY. 221

CHAPTER XVII.

In which Phil and Larry are astonished, and then are astonished again. 235

CHAPTER XVIII.

In which Phil and others solve the Mystery. . . . 249

CHAPTER XIX.

In which Phil and Larry set out on a long Tramp. 263

CHAPTER XX.

In which Phil and Larry visit the Vöringfos in Norway. 277

CHAPTER XXI.

In which Phil rescues Larry from a very perilous Position. 291

CHAPTER XXII.

In which Phil and Larry go through Sweden in the Blanche. 305

CHAPTER XXIII.

In which Phil and Larry meet McFordingham on two special Occasions. 319

CHAPTER XXIV.

In which Phil and Larry finish their Tramps, and settle down for Life. 333

SEA AND SHORE;

OR,

THE TRAMPS OF A TRAVELLER.

CHAPTER I.

IN WHICH PHIL AND LARRY TALK OVER THINGS PAST, PRESENT, AND TO COME.

"HOW are you, old fellow?" shouted Larry Grimsby, as he grasped my hand and wrung it till I could hardly help screaming with pain. "Phil Farringford, I'm downright glad to see you."

"Thank you, Larry; but allow me to remind you that my hand is composed of flesh and blood."

"Is that all?"

"That's enough."

"I don't think so; for I always claim to have some bones in my hand. But how are you, old fellow?"

"Never better."

"And your pa and ma?"

"Excellently well."

"And that little Miss Softwood?"

"Gracewood!" I suggested, indignantly.

"I beg your pardon, Phil. I knew you were just a little soft in that direction; and I had really forgotten what sort of wood she was. Gracewood — I'll remember it now," rattled my friend.

"I hope you will. If you don't, we may quarrel. By the way, Larry, how is that little Miss Pennymore?"

"Fennimore, you rascal!"

"I beg your pardon. I forgot you were rich, and did not need a penny more."

"Very good, Phil. You'll do."

I had come all the way from St. Louis, where my father and mother lived, stopping at Chicago, where my grandfather, uncles, and aunts lived, to New York, in the month of April, to join Larry, with whom I was to sail for Europe as the captain of his yacht. On a similar journey the year before, Larry had saved me from death in consequence of a railroad accident, and I could not help noticing the place on the way where the catastrophe had occurred. We had become fast

friends, because I was able to serve him also. We went to Europe together; and, though he started as a beggar and an orphan, he found his grandfather in the person of Sir Philip Grimsby, an English baronet, of immense wealth; and Larry was now doing his best to spend an allowance of ten thousand pounds a year, which, he confessed, was almost too much for his constitution. We had served on a brief campaign with the French army of Italy during the "battle summer."

On board the steamer, crossing the ocean, Larry had made the acquaintance of Miss Blanche Fennimore, whose mother was connected with the family of the baronet. He was in love with, and now was engaged to her. She had spent the winter with some friends in New York, and Larry had taken up his residence in the great city, in order to be near her. I found him lodged in furnished apartments of the most luxurious description, in Fifth Avenue. He had a large parlor and a large bedroom; and I was glad to see that the former was well stocked with books, which, on examination, proved to be works of history, philosophy, and science. I like to see young men and women read solid works, and resort to novels and stories only for amusement, though they may impart good moral lessons. I was glad to see the character of his books, because we had had some talk on the subject, and he had promised to read good books, and improve his mind. He had written me that he always went to church twice on Sunday, rain or shine; and from what else I knew of him, I was satisfied that he was trying to live wisely and well, in spite of the vast income which he felt obliged to spend. I had asked him in a letter whether he did any good with his money; but he always evaded a reply, quoting the Scripture injunction that the left hand should not know what the right hand did.

I suppose I was vain, like other young men, but I could not help feeling proud of my friend — proud of the influence I had exerted over him. Before I knew him he was dissolute and reckless, whereas he was now a young man of high aims, who indulged in no vices. He had stopped drinking, gambling, and other evil ways, and was, in every respect, as proper a young man as I should wish to see. Somebody has corrupted the old maxim, so that it runs, "Be virtuous, and you will be happy, but, you won't have half so good a time." Larry's experience seemed to be otherwise, for he had "a good time." Well, he had everything to make him happy, including the love of a beautiful girl, who was almost an angel; but then, those who are similarly blessed with all that this world can give, are oftener the ones to turn aside from the straight and narrow path of righteousness into the broad and thorny road of wickedness. I think Larry was happy, and "had a good time," because he was good and true. But I declare I am moralizing; though I believe in this doctrine, and feel inclined to "do it some more."

I told Larry all about the folks in St. Louis and Chicago, and he told me all about those in New York, though I was interested only in Blanche Fennimore.

"Now, how is your grandfather, Larry?" I asked, leaving the most important subject for the last.

"First rate. He says he shall live to be a hundred years old. I had a letter from him yesterday, in which he says Miles has given him a world of trouble during the winter."

"I thought he would," I added. "I'm afraid Miles is as crazy as his father was."

"They say there is insane blood in the family on the mother's side; and Miles senior had it bad before he died. But Sir Philip writes me that Miles has left."

"Left?"

"Gone off in his yacht; sailed, ten days before the letter was written, for the West Indies."

"That's a good place for him to go," I suggested.

"Yes; if he has gone there," replied Larry, with a significant look at me.

"What do you mean?"

"Phil, the more I think of it, the more I am inclined to make terms with that youth," answered Larry, more seriously than he often spoke.

"You have no authority or right to make terms with him."

"I hope the old gentleman will give him half the estates and half the income; and as for being a baronet, I wouldn't give two cents for the honor. Miles can have it."

"But Sir Philip says it is utterly impossible. You can't make a man a baronet by descent who isn't born a baronet. You are the man, and you can't make terms with Miles. You have no right to do so."

"I have been thinking a great deal of this matter, and it has worried me. I stepped in between Miles and his expectations; and it was a tremendously heavy blow to him. It was rough on him."

"But it was not your fault."

"I know that. But I have been considering whether I ought not to sink into oblivion, either by committing suicide, or burying myself in the wilds of Australia, in order to make it all right for this unreasonable fellow."

"Of course you ought to do nothing of the kind. It is not your duty, in any sense of the word, to take yourself out of the way. What would Blanche do?"

"That's where the shoe pinches," said he, with a bright smile.

"Certainly you cannot think of any such thing as suicide, or taking yourself out of the way."

"Suicide is neither comfortable nor pleasant, and I shall not do that. It gives a man a bad reputation. I have always had an idea that I should make my own fortune; and it is rather rough on a fellow to have fortune thrust upon him in this absurd way. I suppose I could go to California, Australia, or some other heathenish locality, and achieve a success for myself."

"One bird in the hand is worth two in the bush, Larry."

"Right! You are a philosopher still, and I'm only afraid you will have an ulceration of the brain, or some other disease in your upper story, if you use it so roughly, Phil."

"I will endeavor to be tender with what brains I have, since it is all there is between us."

He held out his hand to me, and I took it. He shook it gravely, and solemnly bowed his approbation.

"Now, be serious, Philip, and apply your share of the brains to this question. I hope it won't give you a congestion or an inflammation."

"I'm all attention."

"What shall I do with Miles?"

"Nothing."

"What will he do with me?"

"Nothing, I hope."

"I'm really worried about the foolish fellow, Phil. I used to laugh at him; but when I think how much depends upon his getting me out of the way, I don't like the look to windward. Is that perfectly nautical and proper, old Sea Biscuit?"

"Perfectly."

"I don't like the idea of having Miles touch off an earthquake under my feet at any moment, when I don't happen to be thinking of such a thing; or of having him fire off a volcano over my head; for these things hurt; and, besides, it's giving him a heap of trouble on my account, and subjecting him to a heavy expense, for these Italian bravos don't work for nothing."

"I don't think you are very much alarmed about his machinations."

"Machinations!" said Larry, scratching his head, and then grasping the great quarto dictionary on the centre-table.

"From the Latin *machinatio*, meaning tricks, artifices, plots, conspiracies," I added, seriously.

"Thanks. You have saved me the labor of looking out the word. I trust your jaws are still sound and in working order, for you will dine with me to-day."

"You will find they are, for I am half starved for some of your fresh, fat New York oysters."

"They are not very severe on the jaws; but, if you will hold your jaw, I have a word more about Miles. I am really afraid of him."

"Knees smiting each other?"

"Yes."

"Each particular hair on end?"

"Yes; knock my hat off every time I think of him. But don't laugh at my fears. Wherever I go, a quaking skeleton pursues me."

"Not much."

"I should not dare to leave New York, or even to stay here, if I had not you to protect me. Seriously, I am troubled about Miles."

"I do not much wonder. He has proved that he has the capacity for any measure of villany."

"'Any measure of villany,'" repeated Larry, slowly. "Could you tell me where, in Shakespeare, I can find that sentence — play, act, scene?"

"I don't know that it is in Shakespeare at all."

"I was in hopes it was, for it is rather a telling phrase, and exactly expresses my mind. 'Capable of any measure of villany.'"

"That's so."

"Miles intends to shoot, drown, hang, smother, decapitate, garrote, burn, or destroy me if he can. 'To be or not to be,' seems to be the question with me. Assassins lurk in my path — not in

Shakespeare, or the Comic Almanac, so far as I know. Don't you think I had better retire from public life, and shut myself up in a monastery, Phil?"

"Not at present."

I could not tell whether he had any real fears of Miles or not.

"Never mind it now. It's an unpleasant subject, and we will drop it. The yacht is off the foot of Fourteenth Street; and I asked Blanche and her friends to take a sail in her this afternoon. Of course you will go."

"To be sure I will. I am dying to see the craft."

"Don't die yet. Captain Spelter says she is the best thing in New York harbor. I have had her put in first-rate condition, painted, papered, and varnished."

"Papered?"

"Well, I'm no sailor. I had her fixed up; but I havent't the least idea what was done to her. I suppose they papered her."

"Perhaps they did."

"I had her newly furnished, and her cabin is a perfect palace. If she don't sail well, with such a cabin, it won't be my fault."

"What has the furniture in the cabin to do with her sailing?"

"I haven't the least idea," replied Larry, with a blank look. "Then, she has a new suit of sails, fitted by an up-town tailor, I suppose."

"Of course."

"Captain Spelter said they fitted well. Then I had new halyards on the bowsprit, six new spanker booms, four new hatchways, seven new top-gallant jib-stays, eleven new top-bobbin sky-scrapers, and a dozen and a half of foreto'-bow-lines on the cro'-jack catharpings, besides a lot of other things, whose names I can't remember."

"Your memory seems to serve you remarkably well, Larry."

"I have a good memory, when I don't strain it. I paid for so much running rigging that I think we ought to run away from anything that floats."

"I hope she is safe and weatherly."

"O, she is. Captain Spelter says she keeps all the water outside of her."

"Who is Captain Spelter?" I asked.

"He was her skipper last year. He is salt enough to pickle a hundred barrels of salt junk. Is that the sea slang for corned beef?"

"All right."

"It always makes me thirsty to go near him."

"Have you engaged Captain Spelter?" I inquired.

"Certainly not. He was out of a job: I employed him to superintend the fixing up, painting, papering, and getting in the jaw tackle, putting on the barnacles, and adjusting the dead-lights."

"Just so."

"He wants to go in her; but I gently intimated that my friend and fellow-soldier, fellow-sailor, and brother salt, Captain Philip Farringford, was to command the Blanche. Then he wanted to go as prime minister, grand vizier, chancellor of the exchequer, or something of that sort."

"As mate, you mean."

"That wasn't the slang he used," replied my friend, scratching his head. "It was chief executioner, I think."

"I think not."

"Executive officer — that's the slang."

"That's rather a high-sounding title for a yacht."

"Precisely my idea; but, then, I am no sailor."

"Did you engage him?"

"Not I, my hearty! I told him to heave to on the foreto'-bobbin. I was too old a salt to engage any officer without the knowledge of the high and mighty chief captain of the Blanche, my hearty. You see, Phil, he thinks you are a sort of a mud-puddle salt, that don't know the bob-scuttle from the top-gallant spanker boom; and I didn't let on. I suppose you want a chief executioner, or some such bummer — don't you?"

"We want a mate."

"We do, and will have a mate, or die in the struggle to obtain one. Don't have Captain Spelter, if you don't want him. There's sea slang enough in him to fit out the entire mercantile marine of the nation. But I have engaged about a dozen sailors, because they were good fellows, and I didn't want to lose them."

"All right."

"If you don't like them, you can knock them overboard with the main royal bobstay, you know. But come to dinner."

We dined on oysters.

CHAPTER II.

IN WHICH PHIL AND LARRY GO ON BOARD OF THE BLANCHE.

AN epicure in oysters, living in the great west, may become very hungry for the pure, fresh article. I was. Of course the flavor was twice as good because my devoted friend was with me, for the savor of friendship adds itself to the food. We went to the foot of West Fourteenth Street, where Larry made a signal with his handkerchief to the Blanche, which lay but a short distance from the shore. A boat with four oars immediately put off from her, and pulled, man-of war stroke, to the pier. In the stern-sheets, holding the tiller lines, was an elderly man in blue uniform.

"Way enough," said he, as the boat approached the pier.

The bowman promptly boated his oar with the others, and sprang forward with his boat-hook. I saw that the crew were well trained, and those before me looked like first-class men.

"Captain Spelter, Captain Farringford; Captain Farringford, Captain Spelter," said Larry, as the skipper leaped upon the pier.

"Ah, this young man," replied Captain Spelter, as he took my offered hand. "I'm glad to see you, Captain Farringford."

"Happy to know you, Captain Spelter," I answered.

There was a broad grin on his face, and I saw that he was measuring me from head to foot. He evidently considered me utterly incompetent, from the lack of years, to fill the position to which I had been appointed.

"Heave ahead, my hearty," said Larry, as he jumped into the boat. "Is the foreto'-bobbin all right, Captain Spelter?"

"All right, sir," replied the skipper, with a broad grin, for he appeared fully to appreciate the humor of his employer.

"Have you boused the bobstay, and topped up the binnacle?"

"Yes, sir; all done in man-of-war style," answered the skipper, with a sly wink at me.

"Come, Phil, tumble down the hatchway into the boat. Our party will be down here at three o'clock, and we must have all the booms and bobstays overhauled before that time."

I seated myself opposite him on the crimson plush cushions in the stern-sheets while Captain Spelter took his place on the aftermost seat, at the tiller ropes.

"Up oars!" said he. "Shove off! Let fall! Give way together!" and the men pulled steadily, feathering their oars very handsomely at every stroke.

"I say, Phil, how's this for high? Is the foreto'-bobbin all right?"

"I should judge that it was. You have your crew well in hand."

"Ay, ay, sir," replied Larry, gravely. "We have laid ourselves out on this business; and we have the foreto'-bobbin so that it works first rate. There is our craft;" and he pointed to the Blanche. "Isn't she a thing of beauty that is a joy forever?"

"I think she is. She looks like a fine craft."

"She is a beauty, Captain Farringford," added the skipper.

Certainly nothing could have been more elegant or graceful than the yacht, as she sat like a swan upon the water. She had been newly painted, and looked fresh and clean. Much of her rigging was new, and everything was hauled taut, so that she was a model of neatness; and I had a very favorable opinion of Captain Spelter's ability; much more so, evidently, than he had of mine. She had accommodation steps at her side, so that we went on deck with as little trouble as we could have entered a house on Fifth Avenue.

"Once more on the deck I stand of my own swift-gliding craft," said Larry; "only I never happened to glide any in her yet. Captain Spelter has been on a short cruise in her, to see that the foreto'-bobbin was all right."

I examined everything on deck and aloft with a critical eye, and was entirely satisfied with her appearance. Everything was in its place, and every rope handsomely coiled away. The rest of the sailors were on deck, and eyed us with respectful curiosity.

"What do you think of her, Phil?" asked Larry.

"I think she is magnificent; and a fellow that couldn't be happy in a craft like this ought to be shut up in a monastery."

"Just so; and be compelled to live on roast beef, roast turkey, and plum pudding, and omelet soufflé. She is a regular marine sylph. Do you see that dolphin-striker, Phil?" demanded he, pointing at the main boom.

"I don't see it."

"Nor I either. Come below;" and he led the way into the cabin.

This apartment was high and roomy for a yacht. There were two berths on each side, with elegant draperies in front of them, which could be drawn out so as to form a little enclosed space in front of each berth, answering to the purposes of a state-room. The floor was carpeted with tapestry velvet, and the captain said there was a cloth to cover it at sea. In the centre was a table, which could be extended so as to seat ten persons. Over it was a large skylight, which admitted light enough to give the cabin a very cheerful aspect. All around it was a divan, or sofa, covered with green velvet, which was the prevailing color of all the furniture and draperies. Various ornaments were put up in available spaces, and vases, filled with green-house flowers, were arranged about them for the present occasion. In the middle of the bulkhead was a passage leading forward. On the left of it was the owner's state-room, an elegant little room, furnished in bright blue, with a berth wide enough for two. It was provided with every convenience known in a modern yacht, with all those ingenious little contrivances for saving space, which the limits of such a vessel demand. Forward of this was another state-room, whose door opened into the passage-way. It was not less elegant than the owner's, but the berth was not so wide, and thus space was obtained for a desk and case of drawers. Like the other, it was well lighted from the deck, and was supplied with patent ventilators. This room was intended for the owner's favored guest; but Larry told me it was to be mine for our next cruise.

The first room on the starboard side, next to the cabin, was the pantry, which contained marvels of ingenuity for the disposition of the table ware, and for preparing the delicacies for the meals. Forward of this was the cook-room, an apartment twelve feet long by eight in width, with a stove, and every other convenience. At the forward end of it was a door, opening into the larder, which was really an ice-house. From this room we passed into a short passage leading forward. On the opposite side was a third state-room, containing two berths, which was intended for the skipper of the yacht. In the forecastle the berths were rather crowded, for some of them were three in a tier; but there was abundant space for twenty men, as they were accommodated on shipboard. Everything was as well as it could be in the limited space.

"Now, how do you like her, Phil?" asked Larry, after we had completed the examination.

"She is perfectly magnificent. Her accommodations are as good as those of a palace," I replied, with enthusiasm. "She exceeds any idea I ever had of a yacht. We shall be as happy as lords in her."

"I hope so. We have a first-rate cook and two stewards, and we may feed as well as they do on an ocean steamer."

"No doubt of it. And I think she will make your purse sweat, too."

"I hope she will. Why, I paid for her, and three

thousand more for new sails, repairs, and alterations, without making any extra drafts on Sir Philip. And I am not spending all my income yet. I can run her for a whole year on what is left of my allowance, and have something to spare then. But I must go for the ladies," said he, glancing at his watch.

We went on deck, and Larry departed in the boat, leaving Captain Spelter and myself on board.

"And so you are to command this yacht, sir," said the skipper, eying me again from head to foot.

"That is the arrangement I made with Mr. Grimsby," I replied.

"Of course you know that you have undertaken a big job."

"I don't know about that. I shall try to do the best I can."

"I had her last year," added he.

"And you wanted her this year, I dare say."

"Of course I did; but then, Mr. Grimsby told me he had engaged a sailing-master."

"What wages did you get last season?" I asked.

"A hundred dollars a month, for the season."

"How long were you employed?"

"Six months."

"What do you do the rest of the year?"

"Not much of anything; only odd jobs, as I find them. But I don't make a living the rest of the year."

"How much do you want for the whole year?"

"I ought to have a hundred dollars a month."

"That is more than I get."

"I should like to go to foreign parts, and I am willing to go for a year for less, if the yacht finds me all the time."

"It finds all hands. If you will go mate for eight hundred dollars for the year, all right."

"Well, I don't make half that in the clear," said Captain Spelter, musing. "I'll go."

"Very well; consider yourself engaged," I replied.

"But what is to be my position?"

"Mate," I answered.

"Shall you keep a watch yourself, Captain Farringford?"

"That point is not settled yet."

"I don't like to play second fiddle," added he.

"Don't do it, then."

"But I want the place and the pay."

"Do as you like about taking them."

I saw that he had something in his mind which he did not like to utter; but I understood him just as well as though he had spoken out. He did not like to play second fiddle to a youngster like me, was his idea. And when I looked at his iron-gray hair and bronzed face, I did not blame him. Probably he supposed that the entire charge of the yacht would devolve on him; that he would actually sail her, while I took all the credit of it. He doubtless regarded me as a fancy captain, who would live in the cabin and amuse the owner, while he did all the hard work, and kept his watch on deck in a voyage across the Atlantic. He looked me over again from head to foot, and there was something rather contemptuous in his expression.

"Of course I can do as I like," said he; "but I should like to know how I stand on board. Am I to be the actual sailing-master?"

"No, sir, you are not. I am to be the actual sailing-master," I replied, gently.

"Do you think you can take the yacht across

the Atlantic?" he asked, with a kind of incredulous smile. "It's a big undertaking."

"If I could not, of course I should not accept the situation I have taken."

"But you expect to have a capable mate."

"Certainly; one capable of doing a mate's duty."

"One who can navigate the vessel, you mean."

"No; I do not mean that. I mean a mate's duty."

"Have you ever navigated a vessel?"

"I have."

"O! all right, then," said he, with evident surprise.

"If I don't keep my watch on deck, there will be a second mate to do it for me."

"I'm satisfied."

"So am I. And now, as we are to sail, we will go to work. Set the mainsail and the foresail, and heave up the anchor to a short stay," I continued.

My orders were promptly obeyed; but I saw that Mr. Spelter.— as he must be called in his position as mate — was on the lookout to catch me in a blunder. The Blanche was just like any other yacht, and I knew her from keel to truck. By the time we had the fore and mainsail set, and the anchor hove short, the party from the shore came alongside.

"Why, Mr. Farringford, I am so glad to see you!" exclaimed Blanche Fennimore, as I helped her up the accommodation steps.

"And I am just as glad to see you," I replied, grasping her little gloved hand.

"This is a very unexpected pleasure. Do you know, that queer Larry did not tell me you were here, Mr. Farringford?"

"Captain Farringford, if you please, Blanche. He is the skipper of this mighty craft."

"I knew he was to go with you; but you did not tell me he had arrived."

"It was only to surprise you. He has arrived, I'll tell you now. See, the conquering skipper comes."

"As I am skipper, you must excuse me for a time," I added.

"Certainly."

"Take in those steps; hoist up the boat to the davits. Forward, there! heave up the anchor, and stand by the jib-halyards," I continued.

"Ay, ay, sir," replied the hands forward, as Mr.

Spelter went to the forecastle to superintend the execution of my orders.

"Bravo, Phil!" said Larry. "Now top up the foreto'-bobbin, and take a double reef in the flying jib-boom."

"Anchor away, sir!" shouted Mr. Spelter.

"Hoist the jib!" I replied. "Meet her with the helm! Starboard!"

The hands forward ran up the jib, and the Blanche slowly gathered headway.

"Stand by fore and main sheet!" I continued, and two seamen hastened to each of the stations indicated, while the rest, under the charge of the mate, secured the anchor. "Ease off the fore and main sheets!"

The wind was about west, and we had it on the beam. A stiff old quartermaster was at the wheel, and the Blanche went off beautifully. I had nothing more to do at present, and Larry introduced me to the little party he had invited, all of whom, except Blanche, were strangers to me. Requesting the mate to take charge of the deck, I went below with them. I think Spelter was rather surprised, and disappointed, to find I was able to get the yacht under way without asking his advice; but he behaved very well; and, if he had any ill feeling, he suppressed it. The party examined every part of the yacht with interest, and were delighted with her. We went down to Sandy Hook, and had a very pleasant excursion, which I do not intend to describe. On our return we anchored off the Battery, about sunset, near another yacht, somewhat larger than the Blanche, flying the English flag.

CHAPTER III.

IN WHICH PHIL ENGAGES A SECOND MATE FOR THE BLANCHE.

"WHAT yacht is that, Mr. Spelter?" I asked, after he had come to anchor, and furled the sails.

"I don't know, sir; I never saw her before. She's English, but she is a fine craft," replied the mate. "She must have come in to-day, for she wasn't here yesterday."

"Can you make out her name?"

"No, sir."

"I should like to know something more about her," I added. "Get out a boat, if you please, and ascertain her name."

The mate sent one of the two quartermasters on this errand, and I went below — where our party had retired when the yacht came to anchor — to partake of a collation.

"Come Captain Phil Farringford, we are waiting for you," said Larry. "Take your place at the head of the table, where you belong."

"I am willing to yield that place to you, for I believe the sailing-master of a yacht don't always mess at the first table in the cabin."

"He does here. Take your place. You are the Grand Mogul here."

I seated myself in the place indicated, and Larry occupied the next seat on the right. The collation was in keeping with the yacht, and the cook and stewards had evidently spread themselves to the utmost on this occasion, for, besides hot oysters, cooked in all styles, there were boned turkey, ham, tongue, salads, ice-creams, coffee, tea, and chocolate. Everything was as nice as it could have been at Delmonico's. The two stewards, in their white jackets and aprons, were all attention.

"Did you notice that yacht on our starboard bow, Larry?" I asked, when everybody had been helped, and the rough edge of the appetite, stimulated by the sea air, had been taken off.

"On our starboard bow!" exclaimed Larry. "Good gracious! Why didn't you call all hands, and shake her off?"

"Seriously, Larry," I added, in a low tone.

"Seriously, I don't want another vessel on the starboard bow of my yacht; she will rub the paint off, and damage the foreto'-bobbin."

"I think you have spun that bobbin about enough. It isn't nautical, Larry."

"Not nautical! You shock me! Being the owner of a yacht, I deemed it necessary to be a little salt in my remarks, and make an occasional allusion to the skysail boom and the maintop gallant bobstay. The old figure of speech about 'taking a reef in the stove-pipe' I discarded as antique, and inappliable to a nobby yacht like the Blanche, where stove-pipes don't prevail much, though it answers very well for a canal-boat, or a Mississippi flat-boat."

"Did you notice the yacht near us, Larry?"

"'Pon my word, I did not, Phil. Having a captain, mate, and all hands, I can't waste my energies in that direction."

"She is English."

"Ah? And do you think she has any wicked intention of sailing a regatta with me, and maliciously beating me?"

"I don't know about that; but, seeing an English yacht here reminded me of your grandfather's letter."

"There seems to be a very close connection between them. But, perhaps, Phil, if you have anything to say, it will be just as well to say it."

"I sent a boat to ascertain the name of the English yacht."

"Did you? That was a very laudable curiosity on your part."

"Do you happen to know the name of Miles Grimsby's yacht?"

"Undoubtedly I do. I saw the craft at Bristol, and committed to memory her name."

"I am very glad you took so much pains. Here is Mr. Spelter; and probably the boat has returned, with the name of the yacht," I added, as the mate entered the cabin.

"That yacht is the Whitewing, of Bristol," said Spelter.

"Thank you," I replied.

"That's a very pretty name, and I should have chosen it myself, if my yacht had not been already suitably named," replied Larry, without even a start, or any other indication of surprise.

I saw that he did not wish to talk of the matter

before the present company, and I permitted it to drop. After the collation both of the boats were brought up to the accommodation steps, to convey the party on shore. As we were about to embark, a shore boat came alongside, and a man in a seaman's dress stepped upon the deck. He asked for the captain, and was conducted to me by the mate. I judged that he was not a common sailor, for his manners indicated some familiarity with good society.

"This man has been to me, and wants to ship; but, as I did not know him, I couldn't engage him," said Spelter.

"I'm hard up," said the applicant; "and though I got out of the forecastle years ago, I'm willing to take any lay you can give me. I have sailed as mate and sailing-master of an English yacht up the Mediterranean, up the Baltic, and made a summer cruise up to the North Sea."

"I haven't time to talk with you now, but I will be on board to-morrow forenoon at ten," I replied.

"Thank you, sir," answered the applicant, politely touching his cap. "I will be on board at that time."

I rather liked the looks of the man, and I thought

his experience in European waters would be of service to us. He was about forty years of age, and used good language, though he tripped a little on his h's. I went ashore with the party, and, after Larry had escorted Blanche home, I met him again at his rooms.

"Do you know the name of that English yacht off the Battery?" I asked, the moment he came in.

"I do; but I didn't wish Blanche to know that Miles Grimsby was within two hundred feet of her. It would frighten her out of her wits. The Whitewing is Miles's yacht, without a doubt; and she didn't go to the West Indies. I hadn't any idea that she would," replied Larry.

"And you suppose that Miles's errand in the United States relates to you?"

"No doubt of it. The fellow is a monomaniac on the subject of his wrongs, regards me as his evil genius, and, no doubt, considers it perfectly justifiable to put me out of the way in any manner that seems convenient to him, without any respect whatever to my convenience."

"I do not see what he can do, if you are ordinarily prudent, and keep out of his way."

"My self-respect won't allow me to keep out of

his way. I can't go through the world dodging and shrinking from any man. He is my enemy; he has hoisted his colors, and is ready to kill, burn, and destroy me. Phil, I want to be a Christian towards him."

"Certainly; I know you would not injure him."

"I would do more than that; I would be his friend, if he would let me. If he were in trouble I would help him out," said Larry, warmly.

"That is the right spirit."

"Now, as he is here, I intend to see him, and ascertain what he wants. If I can make an arrangement with him, I will do so. I will induce Sir Philip to give him and his sisters a fair half of all the property; and, as for the title, I am willing he should have that, if there is any way by which they can slip it by me. I will see him to-morrow. I'm not afraid of him. I pity him more than I fear him."

"You are perfectly fair, Larry."

"I mean to be; and I shall make a strong effort to have Miles take a reasonable view of the situation. Now, when shall we sail for Europe?"

"As soon as you are ready. I suppose we can get off in a day or two."

"We need not hurry. But you may get everything on board, except the fresh provisions, at once."

"How many seamen are we to have?" I asked.

"A hundred, if you want them."

"Sixteen will make it a very easy thing for all hands."

"Sixteen it is, then. We have twelve."

"Yes; and splendid men they are, too. Am I to keep a watch, or not?"

"How should I know?" laughed Larry. "I want you to make it as easy as you can for yourself. Of course I expect you to go with me on shore whenever I go."

"Then we need a second officer; and very likely that Englishman that applied yesterday is just the man. I shall see him to-morrow."

"Perhaps he is another Cuore," suggested Larry, alluding to the Italian who had been the agent of Miles Grimsby in Europe the year before. "Very likely he came over in the Whitewing."

"No; he was on board of the Blanche several days ago, before the Whitewing arrived," I replied.

We spent the evening in talking over our plans for the future. I proposed a trip up the Baltic for the summer months, and up the Mediterranean for the winter ones, upon which I had studied a great deal before I left home. Larry and I had been studying German during the winter, and he proposed to take a German with us, and continue the lessons on the voyage. We wrote an advertisement for such a person, which appeared in the Herald and Times the next morning.

After breakfast, the next day, we went on board of the Blanche. Spelter was directed to ship four more sailors, and the steward to purchase his stores and provisions for a long cruise. At the time appointed, the Englishman came on board.

"How do you like the looks of that man, Mr. Spelter?" I inquired, when I recognized him in the boat.

"First rate. I had some talk with him, and I know that he is a good seaman," replied the mate.

"Do you think he would make a good second officer?"

"I have no doubt he would. He has been the sailing-master of an English yacht."

The man came on board and saluted me politely

and deferentially, in spite of his age and my youth. I invited him to the cabin, where we seated ourselves at the table.

"Your name, if you please," I began.

"Henry Osborne. I am from Cowes, in the Isle of Wight, and have been among yachts nearly all my life," he answered.

"Have you ever been in anything except a yacht?"

"Yes, sir. I made one voyage to India, and came home as second mate, when I was nineteen. Then I went to China as second mate, and made a voyage to Barbadoes as first mate. After working on shore for five years, I was mate of Lord Gilflyer's yacht, and went for eleven seasons as sailing-master of several yachts."

"You seem to have had plenty of experience."

"Enough to be better off than I am," he answered.

"Why did you leave England?"

"I may as well own it, sir. I got to taking a drop too much, once in a while; and, as no one would give me a position as sailing-master, I went as mate then."

"You don't look like a drinking man," I replied, rather startled by his honest confession.

"I haven't tasted liquor for six months, sir. The liquor is so bad in America, I couldn't drink it if I would; but I have no wish to do so."

"No liquor is served out in this yacht, and I will not keep a man who is intemperate," I added, squarely.

"I intend to be a sober man to the day of my death. I don't drink at all now. Being among the gentlemen, with so much wine and brandy about, I got into a bad way. But, with the help of God, I'll drink no more, sir. It ruined me. And when I could only ship before the mast at home, I came out to America, last autumn. I could not go before the mast; and I had plenty of recommendations from the finest gentlemen in England, who gave them to me before I took to drinking. But in the winter I could only get a situation as a porter in a store. I left my place to go as sailing-master in a yacht a month ago, and spent all my money in fitting myself out for the position. Then the owner of the yacht failed in business, and my chance was gone. I have no money now to pay my board, and my landlady holds my luggage as security for it."

"For what yacht were you engaged?" I asked.

"Indeed, I don't know her name; but she was to sail out of Baltimore, and her owner's name was Mr. McVicker," he replied, consulting some papers which he carried in his pocket.

"Well, Mr. Osborne, I cannot offer you a position as sailing-master, or even as mate, but we need a second mate."

"I am willing to take any place, sir; for I'm hard up."

"This is the owner, Mr. Grimsby," I added, as Larry came out of his state-room. "Mr. Osborne."

The applicant rose from his seat, and bowed low to Larry.

"What wages do you want, Mr. Osborne?" I continued.

"I will leave that to you, sir."

"What shall I say, Mr. Grimsby?"

"Six hundred a year. That's little enough to give a Christian in these times."

"Thank you, sir. That's very handsome; more than I got at home," replied Osborne, with a smile.

"Then consider yourself engaged," I added.

"I am very grateful to you, Mr. Grimsby, and to you, Captain Farringford."

"All right."

"I beg your pardon, sir; but might I beg the favor of a small advance, to enable me to procure my luggage?"

"Let him have a month's pay," said Larry, promptly, as he gave him the money.

"Thank you, sir," replied Osborne; "you have done me a very great favor."

"By the way, do you know this English yacht that lies near us?" I asked.

"It's the Whitewing, sir; I saw her at Cowes last summer; but I was never on board of her. It was said the owner of her was crazy," answered Osborne; "but I never saw him."

"Wasn't it the owner's father who was crazy?" inquired Larry.

"Very likely that was what the story came from. But I have forgotten his name."

The new second mate left the yacht, and Larry and I paid a visit to the Whitewing; but Miles was not on board. We repeated the call every day for a week, without finding him. The sailing-master said he had gone to Washington, but his return was daily expected.

We shipped our four men, and in a week we

were ready to sail, only waiting to see Miles. We
had plenty of applications from teachers of German, and engaged one who had been a clergyman,
and a missionary in Egypt. He spoke English,
French, and Arabic fluently, according to his testimonials, and appeared to be an excellent man
besides. He was poor, and wanted to get home
to Germany. He was willing to serve us without
pay; but Larry agreed to give him fifty dollars a
month, with a berth in the cabin. Osborne came
on board the day he was engaged, and the two
mates occupied the forward state-room together.
He was an exceedingly pleasant man, a good seaman, and a competent navigator. Larry moved
his library on board, and our baggage was in our
state-rooms. We made another excursion down
the bay with Blanche and her friends, and we had
decided to sail the next day, whether Miles returned or not. We came up to the city early in
the afternoon; Larry went home with Blanche, and
bade her adieu, for we had arranged to sail early
in the morning. When he came on board, the
Whitewing seemed to be getting under way; her
foresail and mainsail were set; and we concluded
that Miles had returned.

CHAPTER IV.

IN WHICH LARRY VISITS THE WHITEWING, AND PHIL GETS THE BLANCHE UNDER WAY.

WHILE we were considering the intentions of the Whitewing, a boat put off from her, and pulled towards the Blanche. In the stern-sheets we recognized Miles Grimsby in a Scotch cap. He was paler and thinner than when I had last seen him, and his imaginary wrongs had apparently weighed heavily upon his spirits. The boat ran up to the accommodation steps, and Miles came upon deck. Larry stepped forward to meet him, and extended his hand, which was accepted, though apparently with some doubts and misgivings. I bowed to him, but he took no notice of me.

"I understand from my sailing-master that you have been on board of the Whitewing several times to see me," said Miles; and his utterance was choked and difficult.

"I do wish to see you very much," replied Larry. "I am even in hopes that we can make an arrangement of family matters which shall be satisfactory to you."

"I am willing to meet you alone," added Miles, glancing at me.

"Entirely alone, if you desire it. Will you come into the cabin?"

"Pardon me, but I prefer that our meeting shall be in the cabin of the Whitewing, where we shall be subject to no possible interruption," answered Miles, glancing at me again.

"I assure you, Mr. Grimsby, I will not interrupt you."

"I always find myself at a disadvantage when I attempt to converse with both of you, and I desire to be entirely alone with you, Lawrence."

"Just as you please, Miles," added Larry. "Phil is my particular friend, and knows all about our affairs, as you are aware."

"For that reason I desire to meet you, if at all, on equal terms. The interview is of your seeking, not mine."

"It is, Miles; we are own cousins, and I don't wish to live at war with you. If there is any possible chance to make peace, I wish to bury the hatchet. I will do anything that is right and reasonable."

"Your views of what is right and reasonable are probably very different from mine, and I doubt whether it is of any use for us to discuss the matter," said Miles, who certainly appeared to be more pliable than I had ever seen him before.

"It can do no harm to talk over the matter."

"Very well; if you will go on board of the Whitewing with me, my boat shall return with you when you are ready."

"I will go with you with pleasure, since you desire it," replied Larry, glancing at me, to see if I approved his decision. "But you seem to be getting under way."

"I intended to go to sea to-night, but it is not at all important that I should do so."

"Sir Philip wrote me that you were going to the West Indies."

"He was quite right. I thought to sail for Bermuda and the West Indies to-night, and return to the States when the hot weather came on," replied Miles, in what seemed to be an unnecessarily loud tone, as Larry stood close by him; and I judged that the reply was intended for my information quite as much as for that of my friend. "Are you ready, Lawrence?"

"Quite ready; but as the evening is cool, I will take my over-coat," answered Larry, descending the steps into the cabin.

"Don't you go, Larry," I said, earnestly, as I followed him into the cabin.

"Why not, Phil?" he asked, with a laugh.

"I wouldn't trust him."

"But I am hardly going out of your sight, my boy."

"You know that he is treacherous, Larry."

"But he'll not attempt any foul play right here in New York harbor."

"He'll attempt it anywhere, if there is a chance of success. He has no more idea of going to the West Indies than I have. He came to New York to see you."

"Very likely he did; but the idea of declining to go on board of his yacht here in port, and close by my own vessel, is absurd, Phil. Why, I should be ashamed of myself all the rest of my days, if I were so weak and childish," replied Larry, lightly.

I knew it was useless to talk, and so I did not talk any more. Besides, I had not much confidence in my own position, for my objections seemed to me to be rather ridiculous. I should certainly have gone myself, if I had been in his place.

"Go if you will, Larry; but carry this with you," I added, taking his small revolver from its case in his room. "Put it in your pocket; it is loaded and ready for use."

"You don't think I would shoot him — do you, my Christian friend?" added Larry, as he took the weapon.

"Not unless your own life depends upon your action."

"This is all nonsense; but I will take the thing to oblige you. I don't think I would use it to save my own life."

"I hope you will not have occasion to consider the question whether or not you will use it; yet even the very exhibition of it may be a stronger argument than any other you can use."

He had a pair of revolvers in his room, and without any very definite purpose in my mind, I put the other into my own pocket. We had slept on board two or three nights, rather for the novelty of the idea, than for any other reason; and New York at that time had more than its usual quota of the dangerous classes, and several vessels had been robbed, one of them forcibly, two of the officers being severely injured in the affray with the thieves. We had loaded the pistols for such a possible occasion. When I put one of them into my pocket, I don't know that I intended anything more than to carry it into my room when I went, as I had done before. We went on deck, and Larry got into the boat, in which his cousin was already seated. It was nearly dark when the boat shoved off, and I watched it till the two cousins went on board of the Whitewing.

I felt very anxious about my friend, even while it seemed absurd to me to entertain any fears for his safety. New York harbor was as lively as usual. Sail-boats and row-boats were moving about in every direction, tug-boats were shooting here and there, and an occasional large steamer caused the yachts to bob up and down in the surges produced by its wheels. The revenue cutter lay near, and the scene was almost as lively as Broadway itself. I could not believe that even Miles Grimsby would be so crazy as to attempt any treachery under such circumstances. Still I kept my eye on the Whitewing until only her dark outline could be seen in the gloom of the night.

"An uncommon fast sailer is that yacht," said Osborne, as he paused at the standing-room, where I was seated. "She sailed around the Isle of Wight in a race, and took the first prize; but the wind was very light, and the knowing ones said she could do nothing in heavy weather."

"She must have had some heavy weather in crossing the Atlantic," I added.

"Yes, sir; but they said her best sailing was with a light wind. Your American yachts sail very fast, sir."

"I don't know how they compare with the English."

"If we go out together in the morning, we may have a chance to try a bit with her."

"She is twenty or thirty tons larger than the Blanche."

"But I think the Blanche must be a very fine sailer. Mr. Spelter says she has taken several prizes."

"What is she doing?" I exclaimed, suddenly springing to my feet, as I saw and heard a movement on board of the Whitewing.

"They seem to be heaving up her anchor, sir," replied Osborne, quietly.

I could distinctly hear the rattle of her chain cable, and my heart rose into my throat. I was on the lookout for treachery, and that noise seemed to be the first sign of it. I could just discern the dark forms of the men at work on the forecastle.

"All hands on deck!" I shouted, not very loud, but sufficiently so to be heard all over the vessel.

The order was promptly obeyed, and the men instantly rushed up the ladder from the forecastle.

"What's the matter, Captain Farringford?" asked Mr. Spelter.

"Man the windlass, and heave up the anchor to a short stay! Be lively about it," I answered.

"Are you going to sea to-night, sir?" said Spelter, in evident amazement.

"I have no time for words. You will oblige me by seeing my order carried out without an instant's delay. — Mr. Osborne!"

"Here, sir," replied the second mate.

"Loose the fore and main sails."

"Ay, ay, sir," replied Osborne, with more zeal than Spelter had shown.

I went forward, and sent ten men aft to loose the sails; for we had a patent windlass, which required but few hands to work it. I kept one eye on the Whitewing, and by the time our sails were cast loose, I saw her jib go up.

"Man the mainsail halyards; lively, my men!" I called, nervously, for my worst fears were now confirmed.

It seemed to me that the plan of inducing Larry to go on board of the Whitewing was a contrived one, laid in advance.

"Lively, men! lively!" I repeated; and Osborne hurried the hands to their utmost.

With six men at the throat and four at the peak halyards, the mainsail went up in a few moments.

"Hoist the foresail!" I called to the second mate.

"Anchor apeak, sir," reported Spelter.

"Clear away the jib and flying-jib!" I replied.

At this moment the Whitewing went by the Blanche. The breeze was light, and she moved but slowly against the flood tide. Her crew were setting her gaff-topsails, and I judged by the noise on her deck, that her hands were doing their best.

"Foresail set, sir," said Osborne.

"Man the windlass! Heave up the anchor!"

"Anchor aweigh," said Spelter, a few moments later.

"Man the jib-halyards! Hoist the jib! Starboard the helm!"

"Starboard, sir," replied Butters, the old quartermaster, who was at the wheel.

The Blanche gathered headway, and moved slowly down the bay. I could still see the Whitewing. In a few moments Spelter had secured the anchor.

"Hoist the flying-jib, Mr. Spelter! Get up your gaff-topsails, Mr. Osborne," I continued; and our large crew enabled us to execute all these orders very quickly.

All the hands had been stationed by Spelter, so that when an order was given, it was not necessary to designate the men who were to execute it. The gaff-topsails were brought up from the forecastle, where they were stowed, and hands had already overhauled the halyards, tacks, and outhauls. Though our crew had worked together but a short time, I doubt whether a yacht was ever got under way any quicker than the Blanche.

"Cheeseman!"

"Here, sir," replied the second quartermaster.

"Go forward and keep your eye on the Whitewing, and report every movement she makes."

"Ay, ay, sir."

We had the wind square on the beam, and as we went out from the shore it was fresher than at the anchorage. The Blanche heeled over, and began to go through the water at quite a lively rate; but I could not yet see that we gained on the Whitewing. It was a light breeze at the best, and I judged that the English yacht had the advantage of us.

"Rather a sudden movement, Captain Farringford," said the mate, as he joined me on the quarter-deck.

"Probably you do not understand the situation as well as I do," I replied, hardly able to control my agitation. "I would not lose sight of the Whitewing for all this yacht cost."

"Why, what's the matter?"

"You are aware that Mr. Grimsby, our owner, is on board of her?"

"No! hasn't he returned?"

"He has not."

"I went below at dark, and did not think but that he had come on board again."

"There is treachery," I replied.

"You don't say so!" exclaimed the mate, whose tones indicated utter amazement.

"Did your mate use to ask you if you were going to sea, when you gave him an order?" I asked, for I was provoked with him for his want of zeal after I called all hands.

"No, sir; but then we don't have quite so strict discipline in a yacht as they do in a man-of-war," he answered, sheepishly. "The order was rather sudden, and I was afraid something was the matter."

"Something is the matter; but I don't like to have any one ask me what the matter is when an order is given. The worst might happen while we are arguing the question."

"You are right, Captain Farringford, and I was wrong," he added, so frankly that I freely forgave him.

"All right now; I should not have spoken so decidedly if it had not been an emergency."

"I hope you'll excuse me, captain, for I mean to do my duty, and obey orders, though you are a good deal younger than I am. But I see you know how to handle a vessel; and I know the Blanche never got under way so quick before."

"I am entirely satisfied, for you did your work promptly after you began."

"I'll begin sooner next time. We don't often have any emergencies on yachts, except when we get under way in a race; and then we are all on the lookout. But I can't for the life of me understand this business yet."

"At another time I may tell you all about it; now I can only say that the owner of the Whitewing is a cousin of Mr. Grimsby, and has the same surname—Miles Grimsby. Our Mr. Grimsby is the heir of Sir Philip Grimsby, an English baronet, and stepped between this Miles and his expectations. If he should die, Miles would be a baronet, with an income of half a million a year."

"Whew!" whistled Spelter, significantly. "Then Miles Grimsby wants to get our Mr. Grimsby out of the way?"

"Precisely so; but I don't think any harm has come to him yet."

"Heaven forbid!" gasped the mate. "I understand it all now."

"Then be sure that the Blanche does her best.

You know her better than I do; and if there is any expedient by which her speed can be increased, let me know on the instant."

"She is doing very well now, sir; but the balloon-jib will help her, just as soon as we get the wind a point farther aft, as we shall in a few minutes."

"Have it ready to bend on," I replied, as we went forward.

"Ay, ay, sir."

"How goes it, Cheeseman?" I asked of the quartermaster on the lookout.

"She is gaining upon us a little, sir, if anything."

I examined the position of the Whitewing very carefully, and I was satisfied that the quartermaster was correct in his judgment. She was increasing the distance between us, but I hoped the balloon-jib would give us the advantage.

CHAPTER V.

IN WHICH PHIL DISCOVERS THAT THE WHITEWING GAINS ON THE BLANCHE.

"NOW stand by to start your sheets."

I gave this order when we had run down nearly to the Narrows; and the men who were stationed at the sheets went to their places.

"Run up the balloon-jib," I added.

I did not believe the Whitewing had a sail of this description, and I hoped everything from ours. The English yacht was twenty-five tons larger than the Blanche, and this gave her the advantage. But, on the other hand, she was a light-weather craft; and Osborne assured me that her best sailing was in a six or eight knot breeze. In the month of April we had reason to expect some heavy weather. The Blanche was very broad on the beam, and I had sailed enough in her to understand that she would behave well in a heavy sea, when the wind was blowing a gale. I only feared that the Whitewing would slip away from us when the breeze was light.

The balloon-jib was promptly run up under the drection of Mr. Spelter, who was now as zealous and faithful in the discharge of his duties as I could wish a first officer to be.

"Starboard the helm! Ease off the sheets!" I continued, at the right time.

Our course through the Narrows gave us the wind on the starboard quarter. The immense balloon-jib drew splendidly, and I immediately observed the effect of it in our increased speed. I walked forward to obtain a better view of the chase.

"How goes it now, Cheeseman?" I asked of the quartermaster on duty there.

"I believe we are beginning to gain a little," replied the man. "But I think the Whitewing is getting ready to set a fore square-sail."

"Why do you think so?"

"The hands are at work forward. We are gaining on her, sir," added the old salt, who appeared to watch the situation with quite as much interest as I did.

"Mr. Spelter, we are gaining on her."

"Glad of it. We'll give her some, yet, if she don't slip away from us in the darkness," answered Spelter.

"Get up your fore square-sail, and have it all ready."

"Ay, ay, sir," said the mate, as he called the hands, and proceeded to do this duty.

In a short time he reported the sail ready to be set.

"I don't mean to interfere, Captain Farringford; but I hope you don't intend to set the square-sail yet," suggested Spelter, in respectful tones.

"No. It will only becalm the balloon-jib. But off Sandy Hook we must start the sheets again. If that fellow is going to the West Indies, as he said he was, he will have the wind over the stern. If he is bound to England, as I suspect he is, he will stand off to the eastward."

"Well, captain, I rather think he will take the course that will give him his best point in sailing."

"Probably he will. But this is still an open question to us," I replied. "If he goes to the eastward, we can do better with our balloon-jib; if to the south-east, and right before the wind, we can do better with the fore square-sail."

"That's so, Captain Farringford. I should think you had been sailing in the Blanche all your lifetime."

"But the principle is just as good for any other vessel as for the Blanche."

"I don't know but it is; and I know it is right for the Blanche. We are gaining, captain," added Spelter, with considerable excitement in his manner.

The possibility of overhauling the Whitewing led me to consider the next step. I could not believe that any harm had yet come to Larry Grimsby. Miles was a coward, even in his desperation. All that he had thus far done in his attempts to rid himself of his cousin had been undertaken in the most indirect manner, and while he himself was hundreds of miles away from the scene of action. I was morally certain that he would not resort to immediate violence in New York harbor, or even on the high seas, while there was a possibility of his yacht being overhauled either by the Blanche or by a man-of-war steamer. I could form no idea of Miles's purpose in regard to my friend; but I felt that he was safe from violence for a time; or, even if he was not, the revolver I had insisted upon his taking would enable him to defend himself to the best advantage. The worst that I was willing to imagine was, that Larry was a prisoner in the cabin or a state-room of the English yacht. If the Whitewing went to the West Indies, possibly he was to be released in Havana, and disposed of by a Spanish bravo.

Even if I could overtake the Whitewing, and lay the Blanche alongside of her, the problem would be by no means settled. If we were to fight for the possession of our owner, I was not sure that my crew would "take any stock" in the battle, or, if they would, that our muscle would carry the day; for I was aware that the English yacht had more men. I hoped it would not come to this; but I was ready even for this emergency.

Anxiously I watched the white sails of the chase, and I realized that we were gaining upon her. We were approaching the beacons off Sandy Hook, where the problem of the Whitewing's course was to be settled. We were now within two hundred yards of her, and the question became more exciting than ever. Though I had been through the channel several times, and had carefully studied the chart of the lower bay, I asked Spelter to act as pilot, because he was entirely at home in this locality.

"There goes her fore square-sail!" called Cheeseman, from the forecastle.

"That settles the question," I added to the mate.

"How does she head?" I shouted to the lookout.

"She has started her sheets," replied the quartermaster.

"Then she is going off to the south-east. If she had been going to the eastward, she would have gybed," said the mate.

"It is plain enough that she is going off before it," I added.

"Stand by the sheets!" called Mr. Spelter, when the Blanche came up with the beacon. "Ease off — lively! Up with the helm! Now run up the fore square-sail!"

All these orders were promptly obeyed, and in a moment the Blanche was headed to the south-east, with the wind nearly aft. Half an hour on this course convinced me that we were no longer gaining on the Whitewing, and my heart sank within me. The balloon-jib hardly helped us any; and I had found that our strong point was with the wind a little abaft the beam, with this sail drawing well. But I had the consolation of knowing that we about held our own. I took the departure, and the mate did the same. Heaving the log, I found we were making but four knots. I was confident that we should develop another strong point as soon as we had a fresh breeze; and I hoped we should soon have wind enough to compel the captain of the Whitewing to take in his fore square-sail, which was proportionally much larger than ours, thus giving her a great advantage in a light breeze.

The crew of the yacht had been fully organized, and every man knew his duty. I had directed the mate to have everything done in a seaman-like manner. The bell forward sounded the hours and half hours; all the tricks at the wheel had been arranged, and the crew had been regularly divided into watches, and stationed accordingly. It was no longer necessary to keep all hands on deck, and, agreeably to the old nautical saying, that the captain takes the ship out, and the mate takes her home, the starboard watch, which is the captain's, were ordered to remain on duty, while the port, or mate's, watch went below, to be in readiness to take the deck at eight bells, or twelve at night.

Though my watch was on duty, I was not required to serve with it, for the second mate, when there is one, takes the captain's place in keeping watch. Osborne, therefore, had the deck. I went down into the cabin, and Spelter followed me. I spread out the great chart of the North Atlantic Ocean on the cabin table, and went to work upon it with the parallel ruler and pencil. We were following the Whitewing, and I took from the compass her exact course. Making the allowance for the variation of the needle, I found that the chase was headed for the Bermudas, and had laid her course very accurately for these islands.

"That's clear enough," said Spelter, who had watched my calculations with interest. "If she was going to any point in the West Indies, she would have taken a course more to the southward."

"But she is playing a game; and, when she has fully convinced us that she is bound for the Bermudas, if she can get out of our sight for a few hours, she will change her course to the southward or westward," I replied. "Of course we cannot depend upon anything."

"That's so. A fog or a dark night will give her a chance to dodge us."

"And we can't help ourselves."

"No; that's a fact. She won't show any lights to help us."

"Miles Grimsby said he intended to go to the Bermudas and the West Indies; but he does not always tell the truth."

"He wouldn't be likely to tell you where he was going on this trip."

"Certainly not. And for that reason I am not very confident that he is bound to the Bermudas. But you can turn in, Mr. Spelter. You are wasting your watch below."

"I think I will, captain, for I like to be wide awake when I'm on deck. But I'm perfectly willing to stay up all night if you wish."

"Not necessary. We may as well keep cool, if we can; though I don't expect to sleep any to-night."

"I suppose you are nervous," said he, with a smile. "So am I; and I don't know that I can sleep."

He went forward to his room, and I continued to study the chart for a time. Then I went on deck to ascertain whether we were gaining or losing on the chase. To my astonishment, I found that we were losing rapidly. I was taken all aback by this discovery, for at this rate the Whitewing would be hull down by daylight in the morning.

"What's the matter, Mr. Osborne?" I asked of the second mate.

"I really don't know, sir. Everything is drawing well, and the helmsman keeps her as steady as a vessel can be kept before the wind. I don't understand it, sir. She held her own, at first, for some time. Possibly they have put more sail on the Whitewing."

"She couldn't set another stitch of canvas," I answered. "Go forward, and see if there isn't something wrong."

"She steers uncommon bad, sir," said Butters, the quartermaster at the helm.

"What's the matter?"

"I don't know, sir. Many's the mile I've steered her, and she never behaved like this before. You see, sir, she carries a lee helm now, and she never did it before. I can hardly keep the sails from going over. She feels as though a big whale was tugging away at the lee side of her, to bring her about. I don't understand it at all, sir."

"Give me the helm," I added, taking the wheel.

Certainly she steered in a most extraordinary manner, yawing off when she rose on a billow, with a strong tendency to gybe. I had to meet her sharply with the helm every time she went over a wave. I was no more able to fathom the difficulty than the quartermaster had been. Osborne reported that everything was all right forward. The Whitewing was running away from us with the most appalling ease, and it seemed to me that the pursuit was entirely blocked. I sent the quartermaster to call Mr. Spelter, who promptly responded to the summons. I explained to him the difficulty, but he comprehended it before I had finished my statement.

"I never knew her to behave in this manner before. She acts as though she had a drag, and a heavy one, too, on the lee side," said Spelter. "I don't understand it."

"It is plain that something is the matter, and we must ascertain what it is," I added, impatiently, as I led the way forward, followed by both of the mates.

It was too dark to see anything; but in the waist I observed that the water on the lee side seemed to be disturbed. There was a kind of bubbling and splashing sound, with a break in the sea, which maintained the same relative position in regard to the vessel.

"What is that, Mr. Spelter?" I asked.

"I don't know," he replied, leaning over the rail, to examine the strange appearance of the water.

"Is it a fish?"

"No; I think not," answered the mate, as he took an oar from one of the boats which were swung in-board on the davits.

With this implement he proceeded to punch and thrust at the point where the water was disturbed.

"There! I hit something!" exclaimed he. "It felt like a barrel. "Here, Osborne, bring a boat-hook."

"Ay, ay, sir," replied the second mate, who at this moment was near the lee fore rigging; and he ran to the nearest boat, to obey the order.

"There it goes!" shouted the mate, lifting up the oar. "There's a rope fastened to it!"

I plainly saw a piece of whale-line slide over the oar, as Spelter lifted it.

"She's all right now," called Butters, at the wheel. "She minds her helm like a lady."

"What was it?" I asked, anxiously.

"It felt like a tub, or a barrel, and there was a line fastened to it. Let me see;" and the mate went to the main hatchway. It was the tub we used for lowering small stores into the hold.

"What tub?" I asked.

"It was half a flour barrel, with a rope bail across the top. I put a fifty-six into it from one of the boats this afternoon."

"And it was dragging overboard?"

"Yes, sir."

"But how came it there?"

"That's more than I can say, captain; but it couldn't have got overboard, with the line made fast forward, without help from somebody."

"It's very strange!" added Osborne. "I saw that tub this afternoon on the main hatch."

I inquired of all on deck in regard to the tub, but no one knew anything about it.

CHAPTER VI.

IN WHICH PHIL SPEAKS VERY CANDIDLY TO THE SECOND MATE.

I WATCHED the white sails of the Whitewing with increasing interest. The tub dragging in the water had enabled her to gain at least a mile upon us; but it had fortunately been discovered in season to prevent the utter loss of battle. I was not at all satisfied with the mystery which enveloped the tub, for I could not imagine how it came to be dragging in the water alongside the yacht, with a whale-line evidently made fast to some part of her. I could not but ask myself if there was a traitor on board — some one in the employ of Miles Grimsby. The thought was so startling that it forced me to investigate the circumstance more thoroughly.

I asked all the hands of the starboard watch what they knew about the tub. All of them had seen it on the main hatch, but no one could afford me a particle of information in regard to the manner of its going overboard. I was the more perplexed by these answers. It was half past ten when I went below, and I had not been absent from the deck more than half an hour. Six bells, or eleven o'clock, struck while we were looking for the obstruction to the speed of the yacht.

"Butters, how long did the vessel steer so badly?" I inquired of the quartermaster at the wheel.

"About half an hour, sir," replied the man. "I felt the first drag on me just after you went below with Mr. Spelter, at five bells."

"Did any of the hands come aft?"

"No, sir."

"Are you sure?"

"Very sure, sir. I could see where they were sitting on the forecastle, and not one of them moved. The lookout man was standing on the heel of the bowsprit, where I could see him all the time."

This only corroborated the statement of the watch forward.

"Was any one on the lee side of the vessel?" I asked.

"I saw Mr. Osborne there; no one else, sir."

"Yes, sir; I went over to the lee side several times," added the second mate.

"For what purpose?"

"To get a better view of the chase. According to your honor's instructions, we keep a little to the weather of the Whitewing's course; and I could see her better from the lee side, where the square-sail did not obstruct my vision."

"Of course you were aware that we were losing rapidly?"

"I was, sir."

"Why didn't you report it to me?"

"I was just thinking of doing so when your honor came on deck. I supposed the Whitewing was getting a better breeze than we were, and expected we should catch it every moment."

"That's curious logic," I replied. "Did you expect her to get the first of a freshening breeze when she was a mile to leeward of us?"

"I didn't know but the wind had changed more to the westward."

I did not like the answers of the second mate, and I pressed him still further on the point. He replied that he supposed I had turned in, or he should have reported the situation. I went below, ordering him to call me if there was the slightest change in the relative position of the two vessels. Spelter soon followed me, and as it was nearly time for him to take the deck, he decided not to turn in again.

"What do you think of it, Mr. Spelter?" I asked.

"I don't know what to think of it; but that tub didn't get overboard without some help, I'll wager my year's pay," replied the mate.

"All hands agree that no one but Osborne was over on the lee side after we came below."

"That's a fact."

"And it is rather a suggestive fact."

"Did you mind where Osborne was when I asked him to bring me the boat-hook?" asked Spelter, in a low tone.

"No; but he was some distance from me."

"Well, I only judged by the sound of his voice that he was near the fore rigging."

"What does that prove?"

"Don't you see?"

"I do see; but what do you say?"

"I say that he cast off the line that held the tub.

I have no doubt he had before made it fast to one of the fore shrouds."

"Exactly so; that is my theory," I replied.

We had both come to the same conclusion without any consultation before on the delicate point. It was apparent to me that we had a traitor on board, though it was possible to be mistaken in this, as in almost anything else. He had called me "your honor" two or three times — an expression of which I had not before heard him make use; and it was suspicious at such a time, for an honest man don't toady to any one.

"I don't like to accuse him of this treachery without more evidence," I continued. "But I can't trust him."

"I dare say if you will give him rope enough he will hang himself."

"We can't afford to run out any line to a fellow like him. It looks now just as though he was sent on board to make mischief to our owner. What has he in your room?"

"A valise and a few clothes."

"I will go and see."

We went through the pantry passage to the state-room of the mates. The suit of clothes which Osborne had worn when I first saw him was hanging in the room. I felt that the circumstances justified me in examining his pockets for any evidences of his treachery. In the breast pocket of the coat I found the small blank book from which he had taken the papers he exhibited when he applied for the situation. They were here now, and I examined them again without finding anything to implicate him. In another pocket I found a key, which proved to be the one that opened the valise. This contained white shirts and woollens, but no papers of any kind. As I lifted an under garment, I thought it was very heavy; and unrolling it, I discovered a large leather purse, distended to the utmost with coins. They proved to be sovereigns, and there were not less than forty of them.

"That's pretty well for a man whose baggage was held for his board," whispered Spelter.

"Of course the man is a humbug," I replied, convinced now that Osborne was a "fraud." "But I would like to find some letter or other writing to show his true character."

"There's nothing of the sort here. I wonder the rascal left the key in his pocket."

"Villains always leave some of their tracks uncovered," I answered, as I restored everything to the condition in which I had found it, and returned the key to the pocket.

"I suppose you are satisfied, even without any writings," added the mate.

"Entirely satisfied. It is very fortunate we made this discovery in good time. If I had turned in when you did, we should have lost the Whitewing for this cruise."

"No doubt of it."

"Now, who is your best man forward?"

"Between Butters and Cheeseman there is not much to choose. Both of them are first-rate men," replied Spelter, as we returned to the cabin.

"Which has been with you the longest?"

"Cheeseman; he is an old man-of-war's man; and if he understood navigation, he would be fit to sail a yacht. He was my mate last year."

"He shall take Osborne's place, and have his pay. Are you willing to take him into your room?"

"Certainly I am; there isn't a better man in the world."

"All the port watch, on deck!" shouted one of the hands, as eight bells struck.

Mr. Spelter went on deck, and relieved Osborne, while Cheeseman took the helm from Butters. The second mate went forward, and descended to his room by the fore hatch.

"Are you sleepy, Butters?" I asked, as the quartermaster went forward.

"No, sir, not yet. We have been sleeping in every night since we shipped."

"I want you to answer a few questions before you go below, without fear or favor."

"I will, sir."

"How long was the mate over on the lee side, after I went below?"

"Not long, sir."

"What was he doing there?"

"I couldn't tell, for I was not noticing him. When I have the helm I mind it, sir."

"Where was he when the yacht began to drag?"

"Over on the lee side; but I couldn't see him, sir, for he was between the fore and the main sail."

"Did you hear anything?"

"I can't say I did, sir; but I called to him when she began to steer badly. I told him something was the matter; and he said he could find nothing, sir."

"One more question: how do you suppose that tub got overboard, with a line made fast to the fore shrouds?"

"I haven't the least idea in the world, sir," replied Butters, who was certainly not a swift witness, though he had said enough to convince me, if he had not to satisfy himself.

The fact that Osborne was not upon the weather side when the vessel began to steer wildly was sufficient, with the rest of the testimony. I was too nervous and excited to turn in myself, though I was confident that the mate on deck would get her best speed out of the Blanche. I went below and tried to compose myself. I could not think; I could not read; I could not even keep still. I walked into the midship passage-way. I heard Osborne moving his things in the state-room. He had not turned in, and I opened the door. He was packing the clothes which hung in the room into the valise. I told him I wished to see him in the cabin, and he followed me. Seating myself on a stool at a circular table, on which the chart still lay, I looked up into his face, as he stood with hat in hand before me. His face was pale, and he was not so devoid of emotion as I supposed such a villain would be.

"Sit down," I began, pointing to a stool.

He obeyed me, but in a doubtful and hesitating manner, as though he feared the day of reckoning had come. I looked at him earnestly, to obtain, if I could, any further evidence of his perfidy. He was very much disconcerted, but whether or not this was only the embarrassment which even an innocent person must feel when regarded with suspicion, I could not determine. He did not look me as squarely in the face as I like to have a person do.

"Mr. Osborne, I am not satisfied with your conduct," I continued, when he had seated himself.

"I am very sorry, captain, but I don't think I have done anything wrong," he replied.

"I think you lowered that tub overboard, and fastened the line to the fore rigging."

"I, sir?"

"What I mean I speak out."

"You are very candid, certainly; and if you think I have done anything wrong, I hope you will say so."

"I have said so."

"Would you oblige me by proving what you say, Captain Farringford?"

"I may not be able to prove all that I believe; but I believe it none the less."

"You will allow that it is hardly fair to condemn me without proof, sir."

"I can prove that you have imposed upon me. During your watch on deck, we find that tub, with a fifty-six in it, dragging in the water by a line made fast to the fore rigging. The man at the helm informs you that something is the matter, but you don't trouble yourself at all about it."

"But I did not know what it was."

"I think you did. When you saw that Mr. Spelter was in the way of finding the drag, you went to the fore rigging, and cast off the line. The fifty-six carried it down, and we lost it. It was utterly impossible that any one else could have done this thing. The quartermaster could not leave the helm, and none of the watch forward came aft, or moved from their places at the heel of the bowsprit."

"It is rather hard to be accused in this way."

"Will you explain how the tub got into the water."

"Of course I can't do that."

"You said you saw it on the main hatch."

"I did, sir."

"Do you believe it got overboard without help?"

"Of course not."

"And no one but yourself went near it. If you cannot explain the matter, no one else can."

"Why should I do such a thing, Captain Farringford?" he asked, when he found himself unable to answer me.

"I will tell you why; because you are employed and paid by Miles Grimsby to assist in putting our owner out of the way," I replied, somewhat excited.

"I, sir? Is it possible that you can think me guilty of such a crime?"

"I am entirely satisfied on this point. Of course this scheme to carry off Mr. Lawrence Grimsby was considered before it was put into execution, and you were sent on board the Blanche to make it sure by such a trick as we discovered to-night. This is the whole truth, and of course you know it as well as I do."

"Indeed, you wrong me, sir," he replied, without any excitement or indignation in his manner.

"And you are an impostor, besides. The pretty story you told me about your luggage being held for your board was all humbug. You have money enough to pay your expenses for six months."

"Upon my word, I have only what Mr. Grimsby paid me, less the amount I gave my landlady. I was very grateful to you and the owner for your kindness, for it got me out of a very uncomfortable position. I haven't twenty dollars left; and here it is," he protested, taking his wallet from his pocket.

"Will you open your valise, and let me see what is in that?"

"My valise?" he added, more disturbed than ever.

"No doubt Miles Grimsby pays liberally for such service as you render him, and I am satisfied that you could not have been so utterly penniless as you represented yourself to be."

"I told you only the truth, sir."

"Let me see the inside of your valise, then."

"Certainly, sir, if you desire it."

He rose from the stool, and led the way to his state-room, which was lighted by a gimbal lamp. He unlocked the valise, in which I found he had packed the clothes that had hung in the room at my former visit.

"Search for yourself," said he, stepping back.

I did search for myself, but the purse of gold was not there now. I pulled over every article in the valise, but it had strangely disappeared.

CHAPTER VII.

IN WHICH PHIL DISPOSES OF THE SECOND MATE.

I WAS not quite willing to tell Osborne that I had before examined his effects, nor was I ready to give up the point I had made.

"You see there is nothing in my valise," said the second mate, in a mildly-triumphant tone.

"But do you say that you have no money except what is left of the sum paid you by Mr. Grimsby?" I asked.

"Certainly, I say so. I hope you don't think me capable of a direct lie, Captain Farringford," he replied.

"Whether I do or do not, I purpose to examine your room a little further. If I find that I am mistaken, I shall be even better satisfied than you are with the result."

While I was speaking I looked about the stateroom, in which I was satisfied that the purse of sovereigns was concealed. He seemed to have used his first spare time after the yacht went to sea in putting away his best clothes, and otherwise arranging his state-room. I could not imagine why he had taken the gold from his valise, unless he suspected that I had overhauled his luggage, which seemed hardly probable to me. This room, as I have before stated, had originally been fitted up for the captain of the yacht, and there were plenty of conveniences for stowing away clothing and other articles. I looked into several lockers and drawers, without finding the money, and finally opened the little closet under the washstand. Having had occasion to conceal my own treasure more than once, I not only examined the bottom of the closet, where alone any article could be placed, but I thrust my hand into every corner of the upper part of the aperture. Behind the washbowl, and resting upon the lead pipe which supplied the bowl with water, I discovered what I was in search of. The pipe had evidently been bent down so as to afford a resting-place for the purse.

I was rather afraid that Osborne, when he found that he had lost his case, would turn upon me with violence, though thus far he had been as gentle as a lamb; and I was very careful in my movements. I did not indicate that I had found anything until I had regained my feet.

"Return to the cabin, if you please," said I, finishing the search.

"I don't see in what manner all these proceedings affect me," he replied, backing out of the room, and then following me into the cabin. "I own nothing in that state-room but my valise, which contains all I possess in the world."

"Is that yours?" I asked, throwing the bag upon the table.

"Certainly not. I wish it was," he answered, coolly.

"This is not your money?" I repeated.

"I am sorry to say, it is not. It chinks heavy; if it is gold, it is more money than I ever had at one time in my life."

"Whose can it be, then?" I asked.

"That's more than I know; but I suppose it belongs to Mr. Spelter. I will go on deck and ask him, if you desire."

"Yes; go."

As he went up the steps, I opened the bag, and

discovered, what I had not before observed, his name on the inside of the bag. The second mate was absent a longer time than was required to ask a simple question, and dropping the bag into my side pocket, I went on deck.

"What does he say?" I inquired, when I came to the two mates on the quarter-deck.

"I was just explaining the circumstances to him," replied Osborne.

"The question was answered squarely enough in the beginning," said Spelter. "The money don't belong to me."

"Come into the cabin, both of you," I added, leading the way.

"This is very strange indeed," protested Osborne, as he seated himself in the cabin. "I supposed, as a matter of course, that the money belonged to Mr. Spelter."

"You tried hard enough to persuade me that it did," replied the mate, indignantly. "He told me the money was mine, if I only had a mind to say so, captain."

"Your saying so would not have convinced me that such was the fact," I answered. "I should have thought it very strange that Jacob

Osborne's name should be on a purse of money belonging to Mr. Spelter."

I opened the purse, which was made of chamois leather, and had probably been used for years. I pointed out the name, which was just plain enough to be read. Probably the owner had forgotten this circumstance, as rogues and villains are very apt to make little blunders which betray them.

"Does this convince you that the money belongs to you, Mr. Osborne?" I inquired, pointing to the name on the bag.

"No, sir; certainly not. It only convinces me that my ruin is a foregone conclusion. You are determined to convict me. I hope you didn't write my name in that purse yourself, sir," he replied, with an effrontery which was as cool as it was astonishing.

"Well, Osborne, you are the most impudent liar I ever met yet," said Spelter, unable longer to control his indignation.

"I know of no reason why both of you should seek to injure me."

"You brought that money on board in your valise, Osborne," persisted Spelter. "I saw it there myself."

"Did you open my valise, Mr. Spelter?" demanded Osborne.

"He did not; but I did," I interposed.

"You did?" exclaimed he, pale with anger and emotion.

"I did."

"And I helped him," added the mate.

"Have I fallen among thieves?"

"No; but we have fallen among one thief," replied Spelter.

"Do you consider that you have any right to examine my private property, Captain Farringford?"

"Under ordinary circumstances, no. But when the liberty, and even the life, of my friend, and your employer, are in peril, I regard myself as perfectly justified in doing so. I think I have proved that you are an impostor; that you are conspiring against your employer."

"I have nothing more to say," he answered.

"I have. I will no longer trust you in any position of responsibility on board this yacht. You are no longer second mate."

"Then I am no longer anything," muttered Osborne.

"You can take your money," I added, handing him the bag.

"I am willing to take it, since you insist upon it."

"As you have taken your advance, I shall —"

"As you have made me rich, I can pay you back the advance," said he, taking ten of the sovereigns from the bag and placing them on the table.

"Very well, Mr. Osborne. I ask nothing of you. You are in the employ and pay of Miles Grimsby. Let me inform you that any attempt on your part to interfere with the working of this vessel in any manner will subject you to such treatment as you deserve. I will put you in irons, or put a bullet through you, as the case may require," I continued, toying with the revolver I had carried with me all the evening.

"You can move your traps out of my state-room as quick as you please, for I won't bunk with such a villain as you have proved yourself to be," added Spelter, indignantly.

"Am I to berth on deck?"

"No; in the forecastle," answered the wrathful mate.

"You may berth in the cabin. I prefer to have you here, where I can see what you are about," I interposed. "You will consider yourself a passenger, and have nothing to say to the crew."

I pointed out one of the four berths in the cabin for his use, and he brought his effects from the mate's room. He appeared to assent to all I had said; and in a few moments after Spelter went on deck, he turned in. I was very well satisfied with what had been accomplished, and I rejoiced that we had so early ascertained the treacherous character of the second mate. If I had not gone on deck as I did in Osborne's watch, probably we should not again have seen the Whitewing. He had come on board to do just this work; and if I had turned in, as he supposed I had done, he would have effected his purpose.

I was still too nervous to sleep, and I went on deck again. The wind was hauling more to the westward, and increasing in force. Several pulls had been given at the sheets. So far as I could judge, the Whitewing maintained her relative distance; but the breeze continued to freshen, and at three bells we had it nearly on the beam. The fore square-sail was taken in, and the balloon-jib told tremendously in our favor. Then we began to gain on the chase.

I had already informed Cheeseman that he was promoted to the position of second mate, and he had turned in again in order to be in readiness for the morning watch. As everything was well on deck, I turned in myself at four bells, and I did not wake till six o'clock. I found that the Blanche was considerably heeled over, and appeared to be going through the water at a rapid rate. I went on deck, and saw the chase less than a quarter of a mile ahead of us. Mr. Cheeseman, the new second officer, was on deck, and he was paying the best of attention to the sailing of the yacht. The wind was about on the beam and blowing a ten-knot breeze. It was emphatically lively, for the Blanche had all the sail set that she could possibly stagger under. But she made better weather of it than the Whitewing, which appeared to be laboring badly under her press of canvas.

"We shall be up with her in a couple of hours, at this rate, sir," said Cheeseman.

"Yes; but she cannot carry all that sail much longer," I replied.

"No, sir; she is worrying under it. There she goes, sir! She is taking in her square-sail."

Reducing her sail eased her, so that she went along just as rapidly; for it does not help a vessel to crowd her too much, when it is blowing fresh. She had been driving her bows under, and knocking the water about furiously. We continued to gain on her, however; and when I came up from breakfast with Mr. Spelter at eight bells, we were within hailing distance of the chase.

"We must shorten sail, or run ahead of her," said the mate, who now took charge of the deck.

"Let her drive a while longer," I added.

"What can you do, now you are up with her? Do you intend to lay her aboard?"

"No, nothing of the kind. I don't think we can make anything out of a fight, and we might get into trouble. If we boarded him, he might put an English man-of-war upon our track, or, if we failed, hand us over to the authorities in any port to which he might lead us. I think it is the safer way to proceed strictly according to law."

"But the villain may throw Mr. Grimsby overboard, poison him, or smother him, before we can do anything according to law."

"Well, how would you proceed, Mr. Spelter?"

"I don't exactly know; but it seems to me I should run him down, or lay him aboard."

"If you run him down, you may destroy our friend with the others. If you run alongside, as we can, we shall have to fight it out, and actually capture the yacht, which is dangerous business. No. As long as I can keep near him, I shall be content to wait. But I don't believe any harm will come to Mr. Grimsby while our vessel is in sight. Now, luff a little, and we will run up abreast of the Whitewing."

The helm was put down a little, and a pull taken in the sheets. Our balloon-jib enabled us to have it all our own way, and in half an hour we were squarely abreast of the chase, in a position from which I could have tossed a biscuit on her deck. With an opera glass I examined the persons in sight, but Larry and Miles were not among them.

"Whitewing, ahoy!" I shouted.

"On board the Blanche!" replied the captain of the chase.

"Where is Lawrence Grimsby?"

"Safe and well."

"Will you give him up?"

"No! Sheer off."

At this moment the Whitewing started her sheets, and stood away from us. I told Mr. Spelter to take in the balloon-jib and set the jib and flying-jib. Under this sail we held our own. The chase had come to the wind again, and we continued to follow her. I need not detail our sea work for the next two days, during which time we kept the Whitewing in sight. Sometimes we were near enough to distinguish the faces of those on deck, by the aid of a glass; and I had the satisfaction, two or three times, of identifying Larry among them.

On the fourth day out we had a gale of wind, after a brief lull of the fresh breeze which had favored us nearly all the way from Sandy Hook. It came heavier and heavier, and sail was reduced on each yacht, till each carried only a close-reefed foresail.

We had had a fine run, and according to my reckoning we were nearly up with the Bermudas, and ought to see them before night; for we still held our course, and the log gave us eight knots.

"She is going too far to the westward," said Spelter, after we had made up the dead reckoning; for we could obtain no observation that day.

"That's so. But the fellow is up to some trick," I replied, uneasily; for I had studied the chart with the greatest care. "He has not permitted us to follow him all this time without some purpose in view."

"He means to snarl us up in the reefs off the islands."

"Very likely. He could have done better by running off before the wind; but he has given us our best point in sailing. He means something."

I thought it probable that the captain of the Whitewing knew his way through some of the dangerous openings in the coral reef that stretches out to the northward and westward of the Bermudas. I was soon assured of this by the discovery of breakers on the weather bow. The Blanche was half a mile or more to the leeward of the chase. Suddenly the Whitewing tacked, pitching tremendously in the sea, and stood directly towards the reef. In a few moments she tacked again. I watched her with the most intense interest, for I feared that her captain had outwitted me, and intended to run across the water enclosed by the reef, and come out through some passage known to him on the other side. I told Spelter to come about, but I dared not think of following the chase through the reef.

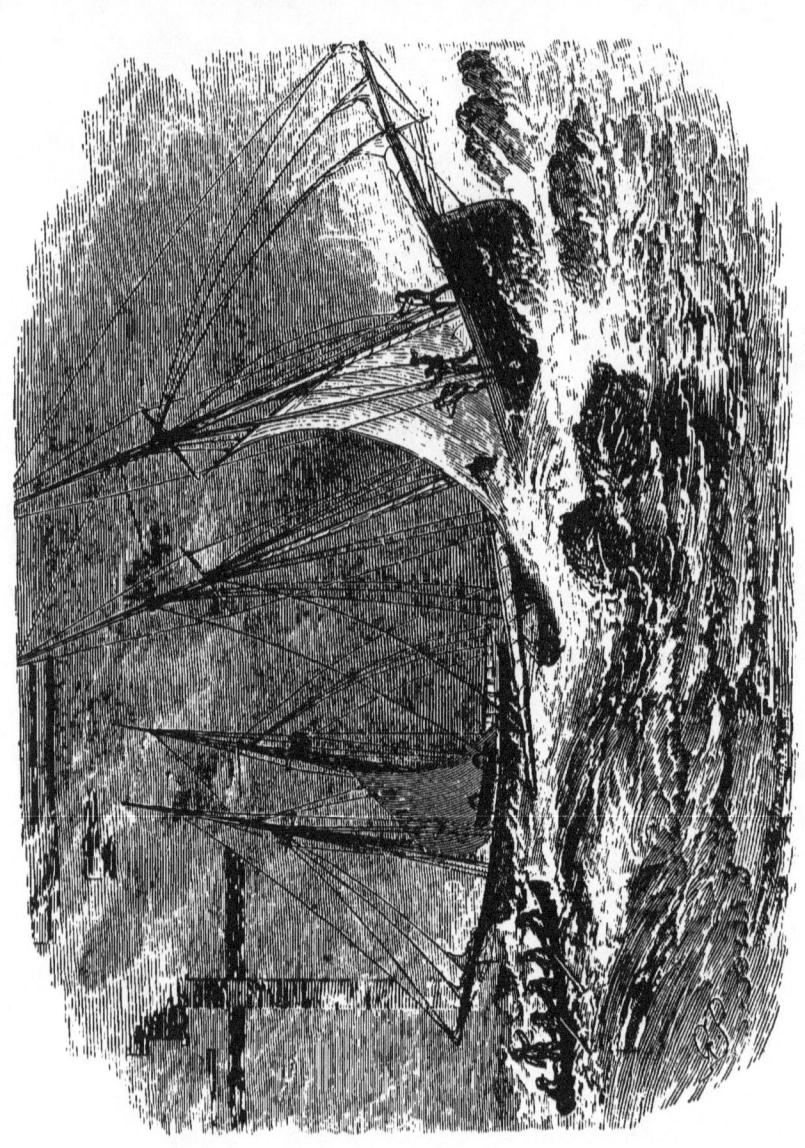

The Fate of the Whitewing.   Page 107.

Suddenly our men forward gave a tremendous yell; and I saw the Whitewing with her bow up in the air and her stern down, so that the sea flooded it at every swell.

"She has struck on the rocks!" shouted Butters.

The captain of the Whitewing seemed to be caught in his own trap.

CHAPTER VIII.

IN WHICH PHIL BOARDS THE WRECK OF THE WHITE-WING.

OF course I was very much startled by the calamity which had befallen the Whitewing, and greatly alarmed for the safety of Larry. As I had seen him on the deck of the chase, I was satisfied that he was not confined below. His chances of saving himself were therefore quite as good as those of the others on board, if he had fair play; but the occasion looked to me like the demon's opportunity.

The gale had evidently passed its height, and was now subsiding, though it was still fierce enough. The Blanche had behaved remarkably well, much better than her English rival. The Whitewing made no attempt to elude us in the darkness, and after the first trial of speed, did not crowd on sail to escape. Indeed, she went along without seeming to care that she was followed, or to realize that the Blanche had the advantage of her. This induced me to believe that Miles had some deeper purpose than was yet apparent.

As soon as it seemed certain to me that the chase would lead us to the Bermudas, I had carefully studied the enlarged chart of these islands. The wind was south-west, and our course was south-east. I had caused a sharp lookout to be kept for breakers on the weather bow; not, of course, that there was any danger from them, but in order to ascertain our position. The Blanche had kept about half a mile to the leeward of the Whitewing. The sea was so stirred up by the gale that we could hardly have distinguished breakers at that distance, if there had been any.

On the chart I readily found the opening in the reef, through which the chase had attempted to pass, and I identified it by a breaker laid down just to the south of it, which appeared only at low water. I consulted my tide tables, and fully satisfied myself in regard to our position. The passage was a most perilous one at any time, but the captain of the Whitewing had attempted it with a head wind, blowing a gale, at dead low tide. I could hardly escape the conclusion that he had intended to wreck his vessel; for certainly he had not more than one chance in ten of going through in safety. But my first solution of the problem was more satisfactory, after a careful examination of the chart — that the captain of the chase intended to dodge through this opening in the reef, where I should not dare to follow him, and, crossing the water enclosed by the perilous reef, — a distance of from fifteen to twenty miles, — pass out on the west side. Doubtless at high water, and under favorable circumstances, he could have safely accomplished his purpose.

"Who is the captain of the Whitewing, Osborne?" I asked, while I was looking over the chart in the cabin.

"Captain Garboard; at least, he was, the last I knew of her," replied he.

"Does he know these islands?"

"Perfectly."

"Not so perfectly as he might, or he would not have attempted that passage in this weather."

"He was in the navy, and served as a pilot on this station. He ought to know all these channels."

"Then he has run his vessel upon the reef on purpose," I replied, hastening on deck again.

The Blanche was approaching the scene of the calamity, going as close to the wind as she could under a double-reefed foresail; but our progress was very slow.

"What do you think of her, Mr. Spelter?" I asked, anxiously.

"She is in a bad way, and if I mistake not, that is the end of her. She must have stove a hole in her bottom, and she seems to be bumping heavily on the reef. I see they are trying to work her off. There she bumps again!"

"They are clearing away a boat," I added.

I watched them with interest, as the seamen of the Whitewing lowered the boat into the water. It hung at the davits on the weather side. A wave came up under it, and tossed it across the quarter-deck of the vessel. I thought I could hear the crash of planks as it struck the rail; but whether I did or not, the boat was stove. Another sea swept it away, for it was no longer worth retaining.

Ours were both life-boats, built of iron. Four men had already been detailed to pull one of them. They were the ablest and best seamen on board, and I had the fullest confidence in them. I had decided to go with them myself, and to take the mate with me, for other questions than those relating to seamanship were liable to come up for settlement.

"I think we had better not go any nearer," said Spelter.

"Heave her to, then," I replied.

The fore-sheet was hauled down till the double-reefed foresail was as flat as we could make it. Butters was placed at the helm, for he was the most experienced hand.

"Clear away the starboard quarter boat!" I continued. "Man the falls!"

When the life-boat was swung out on the davits, the four men took their places in her. I took my position in the stern-sheets, and Spelter in the bow.

"Now mind your eye, Butters," I shouted, when we were all in our places, and the seamen had their oars up.

"Ay, ay, sir!" responded the helmsman.

"Let her off a little!"

A big sea lifted the yacht, and the wind heeled her over.

"Lower away!" I cried at the top of my lungs, for the sea made a tremendous noise.

Promptly the hands at the falls on deck lowered the boat till it struck the receding sea beneath.

"Cast off the falls," I added to Spelter, and I unhooked the one in the stern.

The great billow swept us away from the yacht, as Butters put the helm down, and threw her head up to the wind again.

"Let fall! Give way together!" I continued; and the seamen dropped their oars into the water, and began to pull a steady, strong stroke all together.

Grasping the tiller ropes, I threw the boat's head up to the sea, as a big wave lifted us up into the air. Spelter crawled aft, and we trimmed the boat between us. I had not permitted her to get into the trough of the sea, where she would certainly have been overturned; for a life-boat will upset as easily as any other craft. The sea combed in over the bow and stern, and in a few moments all hands were wet to the skin, and the water was swashing fore and aft in the bottom of the boat. The men pulled admirably, and there was no jerking or irregularity in their movements. Every oar seemed to do its part in keeping the boat steady.

The Whitewing had run up close to the reef, and then tacked to the southward — a course which brought her into the jaws of the passage. On this tack she had run upon the reef, and consequently lay with her head to the southward, the wind raking diagonally across her deck. As we came near her, I heard her planking and timbers snapping and grinding on the reef, the sea making a clean breach over her quarter-deck.

"It's all over with her," said Spelter. "The bottom is all knocked out of her, and she is all afloat inside."

"It was madness to go into such a place as this in a gale of wind," I added. "The worst of our job is yet to come."

"That's so. If some of those fellows don't lose the number of their mess, I am mistaken."

"I hope we shall be able to save them all."

"I hope so, too; but if any one is to be lost, I hope it will be the right one."

By this time we were within hail of the people on the wreck, who were all gathered in the forecastle, holding on to the fore rigging, and to the life line, which had been stretched across the deck.

"Swing out your main boom!" I shouted.

"That's easier said than done," added Spelter. "The sea is making a clean sweep over her quarter-deck."

"They are going to try it, at any rate. I think I could do it, if I were there."

"So could I; but those people seem to be rather demoralized. If they do it in as lubberly a manner as they attempted to get their weather quarter boat overboard, they won't succeed."

"Lay on your oars, men! Pull steady, and keep her head up to it," I called to the oarsmen.

"There he goes," said the mate, as one of the seamen on the deck of the Whitewing, taking advantage of a lull in the sea, rushed aft, carrying a rope in his hand.

Passing it outside of the lee main shrouds, he reached the main sheet, just as another sea swept over the stern of the vessel. Fortunately it was not so heavy as many others had been, and holding on at the sheet he saved himself from being washed overboard. In desperate haste, he made fast the end of the rope he had carried aft to the boom. He then cast off the main sheet, as another sea boarded the stern; but he leaped upon the boom, and held on at the topping lift, by which he raised himself above the burden of the angry billow.

"Sway away!" shouted the brave fellow, as he raised the boom by heaving on the topping lift.

The hands forward hauled on the guy rope he had attached to the boom, while the seaman overhauled the main sheet, so as to permit it to run out. He maintained his place on the spar, and in a few moments was out of the reach of the seas that swept over the stern. It was exceedingly well done on his part.

"Now give way, my men," I continued, when the boom was swayed out so that it was in range with the direction of the wind.

In a few moments our boat was under the lee of the Whitewing's stern, which to a considerable extent broke the force of the heavy seas. The bow was run up under the boom. The man on this spar had hauled out the end of the sheet, and having secured the boom where it was, so that it could not swing forward or aft, he dropped the rope into the boat, where it was secured by our bowman, and the brave fellow above was the first to descend.

"God bless you for what you eave done!" exclaimed he.

"What is the condition of your vessel?" I asked.

"Full of water, sir."

"Where is Lawrence Grimsby?"

"Who?"

"The passenger, I mean."

"Indeed, sir, I fear he is lost, sir."

"Lost!" I cried, aghast at this answer.

"He was not among the rest of the people. I think he was in the cabin, sir," replied the sailor.

"Avast there!" I yelled, as loud as I could speak, when I saw some of the people of the Whitewing mounting the boom, Miles Grimsby among the number. "I want Lawrence Grimsby first."

"He is lost!" shouted the captain of the Whitewing.

"Can it be possible?"

"The cabin is full of water, sir," replied the English seaman.

I was maddened at the thought. Springing

forward, I grasped the sheet, and climbed upon the boom.

"Cast off, and go astern a little, Mr. Spelter," I called to the mate. "Don't take in a single one till I give the order."

"Ay, ay, sir."

I crawled on the boom down to the mainmast, and leaped upon the deck.

"Where is Lawrence Grimsby?" I demanded, above the howl of the storm, as I confronted Miles.

"Really, I don't know," replied Miles, his teeth chattering with terror.

"I haven't seen him since we struck," added Captain Garboard.

"He was in the cabin," muttered Miles.

"Did you mean to drown him," I cried, hardly able to keep my hands off the villain's throat.

"No, no!" pleaded Miles. "I meant him no harm."

"Where is he?"

"He was in the cabin."

"And the cabin is under water!" I gasped. "Where was his room?"

"On the starboard side."

This answer, if it was correct, made the matter

more hopeful. I ordered the captain, in the most peremptory tone, to conduct me to the cabin.

"Not a man shall be saved, if he is lost!" I added.

"I think he is safe," replied Captain Garboard. "I didn't think anything about him after we struck, for then it was every man for himself."

He led me into the forecastle, and then through various rooms, till we came to a passage by which the cabin was reached. The water was three feet deep amidships, but as the vessel was heeled over to port, her starboard side was not so low in the water.

"Help! Help!" shouted Larry.

"He has that room on the starboard side," said the captain.

The key was in the door, and the door was locked. I turned it, and found my friend up to his knees in the water, holding on at his berth. I folded him in my arms and wept with joy.

"I didn't think I should ever see you again, old fellow," said he.

"Come with me, but be careful," I added, leading him by the hand through the water, to the forecastle.

We ascended to the deck, where Miles was waiting in terror and anxiety for our appearance. I took no notice of him, but conducted Larry to the boom, where I bade him follow me. As the sail was secured on the spar, the passage was not very difficult, though we were drenched with spray. As soon as Spelter saw me the boat came up to the boom, and was made fast by the rope. I assisted Larry to descend, and rejoiced when I saw him safely in the boat. I followed him, but the moment I was in the boat, I cast off the rope.

"Pull, port! back, starboard!" I shouted.

The boat came about very well under the lee of the wreck, and the movement was followed by a howl of dismay from those on the Whitewing.

"Save me! save me!" yelled Miles Grimsby, in the most abject terror, from the boom on which he had perched himself.

"Be patient!" I replied.

"Surely you will not let our people perish," interposed the English sailor in the boat.

"No; but I will not expose my friend whom that miscreant would have murdered, to any risk, if I can help it. The boat shall return at once," I replied.

I was afraid the people on the wreck would crowd the boat so as to endanger her safety, and I was determined to make sure of Larry before I attempted to save those who had kidnapped him. The Blanche had fore-reached so that she had diminished the distance between herself and the wreck one half. We ran under her stern, and Larry, the English sailor, and myself, climbed on board by a rope dropped from the main boom. I directed Spelter to return to the wreck, and bring off as many as he could safely of her crew.

CHAPTER IX.

IN WHICH PHIL TAKES MILES GRIMSBY AND OTHERS ON BOARD THE BLANCHE.

AS the gale was blowing less fiercely now, I brought the Blanche over on the other tack, and lowered the port quarter boat into the water, with another crew under Butters to assist in bringing off the people of the Whitewing. I was delighted with the working of our boats, for they had been purchased at my suggestion. I did not like the light and frail structures, which answered very well for ordinary yachting, and they had been discarded. I could not help thinking that the present safety of our owner was in some measure due to the excellent character of our boats, for the cockle shells we had left in New York, in which two men pulled four oars double-handed, could not have been very serviceable in the raging sea that now prevailed. The port quarter boat behaved quite as well as the other, under the skilful management of Butters; and I could see no reason why every man on the wreck should not be saved.

But all this time I was nursing my indignation against Miles Grimsby and the officers of the Whitewing for their infamous conduct towards Larry. Miles had been utterly treacherous, and I had lost all hope of any reconciliation between the cousins, if I had ever cherished any. While I was considering the subject, and trying to feel like a Christian towards our enemy, Larry, who had gone below to obtain dry clothing, came on deck. I had hardly spoken a word with him yet about the events which had transpired since we parted in New York Bay. It was enough for the present that he was safe; and I was determined that he should not again trust himself, even for an instant, in the hands of his wicked cousin.

"I hope you are doing all you can to save the people of the Whitewing, Phil," said he.

"I am; but I am willing to own that I haven't much heart in the job," I replied.

"Why not?"

"Because Miles has been so infamously treacherous to you. Why, the wretch locked you up in your room so that you might perish there, like a felon in his cell."

"You are a little too fast, Phil. He didn't do that. But suppose he had done it, and suppose I had been drowned when the yacht first struck; would it have been any the less your duty to save Miles and the crew of the Whitewing? Will you answer this conundrum?"

"Of course it would have been my duty to save all the survivors; but I should not have relished the undertaking half so well as if they were honest men."

"Perhaps not. I have been more afraid of losing my soul than of losing my body. I have been locked up in that state-room for two days. The only book I had was the Bible, for I found one in the room, placed there by a Bible Society, as I learned by the inscription on the cover. When we get to London, I'm going to give a thousand pounds to that society, for those two days with the Bible did me more good than all the reading I ever did before in my life."

"But we have read the Bible a great deal together."

"I know that. But you see, Phil, it was the peculiar circumstances that forced its blessed truths right home to my conscience and to my heart. In London, Liverpool, and elsewhere, I have seen these same Bibles in the rooms of the hotels, and have even read them; but I was not exactly in the mood to be influenced by the teachings of the book, as I have been for the last two days. I used to think it was all nonsense to put the Bible in steamboats, hotels, and other public places, for my observation was, that no one ever looked into them, unless it were pious people, who always carried it with them. But if one in ten thousand of those distributed affords as much comfort and consolation to a single reader as mine did to me, it is a splendid interest on the investment."

I was astonished at the remarks of my friend at such a time; and I confess that they moderated my indignation towards Miles and his companions. But I had no time to consider his views then, for Mr. Spelter's boat was approaching, and it was necessary to get the Blanche in position for taking her passengers on board. In the stern-sheets sat Miles Grimsby, holding on with both hands like a frightened child. The boat came up under the stern of the yacht, and the bow-man seized the rope which was thrown to him. The English sailors came up without difficulty, but Miles was clumsy and unskilful. After the first trial he dropped down into the boat, unable to climb up the rope to the main boom.

"Up with you," shouted Mr. Spelter, savagely. "Don't keep us waiting here all day."

"Not a word, Mr. Spelter!" Larry interposed, warmly. "Don't you see he can't climb that rope?"

"Then let him go overboard, and be hanged to him," responded the indignant mate.

"Save me! save me!" moaned Miles, terrified still more by the harsh words of the mate.

"If you let him go overboard, Mr. Spelter, I'll discharge you," cried Larry. Come, Phil, what is to be done? We must get Miles on board, if we don't anybody else."

"All right; we can get him on board easily enough," I replied.

I sent a hand out on the boom with a snatch-block, which I directed him to make fast to the topping-lift. A rope was passed through this block, and one end lowered into the boat, the other end leading to the quarter-deck.

Miles Grimsby in Slings. Page 127.

"Make a sling in the rope, Mr. Spelter," I called to the mate; "see that everything is secure, and get him into it."

The mate quickly obeyed my order, and in a moment Miles was seated in the sling, holding on at the rope with his hands.

"Now, walk away," I added to the men on the quarter-deck who had been stationed at the rope. "Steady! Don't hurry."

I went out on the boom myself, and swayed off the rope, so that Miles might not be jammed on the spar, and in a moment he was hauled up to the topping-lift.

"Lower away," I continued, taking the feet of Miles and separating them, so that he came down astride of the boom. "Now work yourself inboard, Mr. Grimsby."

I kept behind him, and held him so that the violent motion of the Blanche should not unseat him, and he hitched slowly along till Larry grasped him by the hands and assisted him to the deck.

"Give me your hand, Miles," said my friend, as he grasped that of his trembling cousin. "I congratulate you on your safety."

But Miles could not speak. He was drenched to the skin, and shaking with cold as well as with fright.

"Come into the cabin, Miles, and we will soon make you comfortable," continued Larry, taking Miles by the arm and conducting him as tenderly as though he had been his best friend, instead of his most bitter enemy, to the companion-way. They disappeared in the cabin; but I heard Larry calling for the cook and the cabin steward, who were on deck rendering what help they could. Mr. Spelter went off to the wreck again, and he had hardly left before the other boat came up under the boom. In another hour every one of the people on board of the Whitewing was safe. Captain Garboard came in the last boat. The mainmast of the wrecked vessel had gone by the board, the stepping having been ground away by the motion of the hull on the reef. It tore up the deck as it fell, and I was satisfied that in a few hours more there would be nothing left of the Whitewing. Our boats were hoisted up, and I directed Cheeseman to fill away on our course again.

I invited Captain Garboard into the cabin, and

all the rest of the Whitewing's crew had gone to the forecastle. Going below myself, I found that Larry had clothed Miles in a dry suit of his own, and had actually installed him in his own state-room. The steward was just bringing in hot coffee and other refreshments.

"I hope you feel comfortable now, Miles," said Larry.

"Better," replied Miles.

"Now take a cup of coffee; it will warm you."

"Thanks," muttered the guest.

"You will join us, Captain Garboard," added Larry. But you must have dry clothes first."

"But I don't happen to have any. I have lost every stitch I had," answered Captain Garboard, gloomily. "It makes no difference to me. I am used up for this world."

"Not quite. But you shall be made comfortable while you are on board of the Blanche," added Larry.

Osborne, who was about the size of the captain, offered a suit for his use, and, retiring to my room, he put it on. The steward brought in for the table the best the yacht afforded, and Larry dispensed his hospitality with the most liberal hand. He was gentle and assiduous in his efforts to make his guests at home; but both of them were sullen and silent. I could not see that his extraordinary zeal and kindness had any effect upon Miles, though he often expressed his thanks in a single word. I had looked in vain for any signs of recognition when Osborne met Miles, but of course both of them were too cunning to betray their own treachery.

The scene of the wreck of the Whitewing was within a few miles of St. George, the most northern of the Bermudas; but the weather was so thick to windward that we could not see it. As it was now nearly night, I decided to stand off till morning, and then, if the weather was suitable, to go into St. George's harbor. The gale was subsiding, and the wind hauling to the northward. As we were under the lee of the islands, the sea was tolerably smooth. We had taken in the foresail, and were now under jib and reefed mainsail. The yacht was crowded by the addition of the crew of the wrecked yacht; but our men gave up their berths to the Englishmen without an exception; and those who could not have berths were accommodated on the divans and the floor of the cabin.

After supper, Miles complained of not feeling well, and wished to retire; but I was satisfied that this was only an excuse to get rid of the company of his cousin, whose kindness, instead of touching his heart, seemed to disgust him. Captain Garboard was silent and moody, though I could not help talking to him; and I finally unsealed his lips, so that he was willing to speak of the disaster which had destroyed his vessel.

"That was a dangerous passage through which you attempted to pass," I began, as we were all seated in the cabin.

"Yes."

"And you did not choose the most favorable time for attempting it," I added.

"No."

"Was it your own or Mr. Grimsby's plan to go through that passage?"

"My own."

"I suppose you intended to get away from us by that course."

"Yes."

"It was an unfortunate move for you," I persisted.

"Yes, very."

"But I should have followed you through, if the weather had been suitable."

"Then you would have been where we are now," replied Captain Garboard, rather sharply.

"Well, that is precisely what you desired, I suppose."

"No, not that. If you mean to say that I am just as big a villain as"—he pointed to Larry's state-room, in which Miles had turned in—"you are right. I am. I am properly served out for what I have done."

"But what was your object in going through that dangerous passage?" I asked.

"Simply to shake you off; nothing more, upon my conscience. Perhaps I am not so bad a man as you think I am."

"I hope not," I answered candidly. "But did you not expect me to follow you?"

"No. I knew you could not be so reckless. I intended to make a harbor inside the reef, after I had shaken you off, and run out on the other side when the weather favored. I have been a pilot among these islands, and know every channel and rock."

"But you certainly mistook the channel through which you attempted to pass."

"No, I did not. It was the vessel's fault, not mine. She didn't work well under her close-reefed foresail, and when we went in stays, she wouldn't come about, but jammed her head right on the reef. I have been through that passage in a schooner several times under precisely the same circumstances; and if we hadn't been serving the devil, instead of a Higher Power, I should have taken her through all right this time," he added, dropping his voice to a low tone.

"You seem to have a proper appreciation of the work in which you were engaged, Captain Garboard," I replied.

"I have; and I understood it just as well before as I do now."

"Why did you do it then?"

"What could I do? I am a poor man, dependent upon my situation for the support of my family. I could only do what my owner bade me, or leave his employment. I don't often obtain a winter job."

"I suppose you know Mr. Osborne, here," I added, indifferently.

He glanced at our late second mate, but seemed to be in doubt about answering the question.

I told you I had seen him at Cowes," said Osborne.

"Half the truth's a lie," added Captain Garboard. "He was the first mate of the Whitewing, and crossed the Atlantic in her."

"I hadn't much doubt of that," I replied. "But he betrayed himself before we were six hours out of New York."

For the benefit of Larry and the English captain I repeated the story of the tub. Osborne did not resent the exposure, probably feeling that he was already convicted.

"I suppose you knew Osborne when he drank too much," I continued.

"I never heard that he was an intemperate man," replied Captain Garboard.

"Because I never was," added Osborne. "I can wipe that stain out of my character, if I can't the other. But, like the captain, I had to obey the orders of the owner, and I don't often get a winter job."

"That's a poor excuse, I think. A man had better go to the workhouse than sacrifice his honor and integrity," I observed.

"True. I believe it now, if I never did before."

"But the gravest charge that can be brought against you is the locking up of Mr. Lawrence Grimsby in his state-room, where — "

"Avast there, Phil. Just clap a stopper on the foreto'-bobbin," interposed Larry. "I have told you I was in that state-room for two days, and therefore I couldn't have been locked in for such an occasion as the wreck of the Whitewing. Don't make it any worse than it is."

"It's bad enough, any way."

"So much the more reason for not making it any worse. In due time I will tell my own story," added Larry.

"Suppose you begin now," I suggested.

"All right. Here goes. When I left you in New York harbor, Miles seemed to be very pliable, and I had high hopes — "

"Sail, ho!" shouted Mr. Spelter, opening the cabin door. "There's a schooner on our lee bow, Captain Farringford. She has just fired a gun; there goes another. She seems to be in distress."

"Run down to her," I replied, hastening on deck, followed by all in the cabin.

CHAPTER X.

IN WHICH PHIL RELIEVES THE HERMIA, AND LISTENS TO LARRY'S STORY.

"WHAT do you make of her, Mr. Spelter?" I asked, as I joined the mate on deck.

"The guns indicate that she is in distress; but she seems to be well up in the water, and works very well," replied the mate.

The clouds had rolled away, and the sky was clear now. It was not very dark, and we could make out the schooner's appearance quite distinctly as we approached nearer.

"She is no merchant vessel," said Spelter. "She is a trim-built craft, and trimly rigged."

"I think she is a yacht," added Captain Garboard.

"That's my idea," responded the mate.

"Two English yachts that I know of sailed for the West Indies in October, their owners intending to winter among the islands. I think this vessel is one of them, for she looks like an English-rigged yacht," continued Captain Garboard. "One of them was the Hermia, belonging to Mr. Fitzgerald, and the other was the Japonica, owned by Mr. Golding."

We ran under the stern of the stranger, and came up into the wind, as she had done before. There was no appearance of anything wrong about her, for she had not lost a spar, and her jib and mainsail were set.

"Schooner, ahoy!" shouted Mr. Spelter.

"Schooner, ahoy!" replied some one from the stranger.

"What vessel is that?"

"The Hermia, of Southampton, in distress."

"What's the matter?" demanded Spelter.

"We are short-handed, and want a navigator. Can you help us?" inquired the spokesman of the Hermia.

"Ay, ay! Send a boat on board."

"Short-handed," repeated Captain Garboard. "She was that when she left England. She took only eight men besides the captain, who was the only navigator on board. The owner was careful of his pocket."

The boat from the Hermia soon came alongside, and the officer who had come in her leaped on our deck.

"Is that you, Graves?" asked Captain Garboard, approaching him.

"No, sir. My name is Finch," replied the man.

"But where is Captain Graves?"

"He was lost overboard yesterday, with the mate and three seamen, in the hurricane."

"Poor Graves!" sighed Garboard. "I knew him well, and he was a good fellow. Is Mr. Fitzgerald on board?"

"Yes, sir. He is very anxious and uneasy, for we have but four men left, besides the cook and steward."

"I should think he might be, if he has no navigator on board," added Captain Garboard.

"We lost a man by sickness in Havana, and we sailed for England one hand short. Yesterday morning the wind was fresh and increasing. We were under jib and reefed mainsail, when it suddenly came down upon us in a hurricane. We had the reefed foresail ready to set, and had luffed up to get in the mainsail, when the wheel got jammed by the sail coming upon it, and the vessel fell off into the trough of the sea. Just at that moment a tremendous sea boarded us on the quarter-deck, and the captain, mate, and three seamen were swept away. I am the second mate; and I had hauled down the jib, and was getting the reefed foresail up at the time. We rolled at the mercy of the waves for a few minutes, for I could do nothing. When the wind eased off, I set the foresail and secured the mainsail. I got her out of the trough of the sea, but for four hours I thought that every moment would be our last. I looked about me for the captain and the others who had been swept overboard, but I could not see them. Both of our boats were carried away, but we received no material damage."

"Where was Mr. Fitzgerald all this time?" asked Captain Garboard.

"Shut up in the cabin, sir, expecting every instant to go to the bottom. I lashed myself to the wheel, or I should have gone overboard. I am no navigator, sir, and I haven't the least idea where I am."

"You are just to the eastward of the Bermudas."

Every person on board of the Blanche, except

Miles Grimsby, had come on deck when the intelligence of the vessel in distress was circulated. Captain Garboard and Osborne both offered their services to navigate the Hermia to England; and I soon ascertained that every one of the Whitewing's crew was anxious to go home in the yacht. They had lost their voyage; and if I landed them at the Bermudas they might be obliged to remain there for weeks, and even months, before they could return to England. It was therefore a matter of the deepest interest to them, and they were very strenuous in their demands. It was finally decided that Captain Garboard and Osborne should go on board of the Hermia, and arrange for the passage of the entire crew. In half an hour they returned with the intelligence that Mr. Fitzgerald agreed to take the whole crew of the Whitewing, Garboard as captain, Osborne as mate, and the rest to work their passage.

"Where is Mr. Grimsby?" asked the captain.

"He is in his state-room still," I replied. "He has not been out of it. Do you wish to see him?"

"No. I hope I shall never see him again."

"But do you intend to leave without saying good by to him?" I inquired.

"I do. If your Mr. Grimsby can forgive me for the injury I have done him, I shall be happy."

"There's my hand," interposed Larry. "I don't think you ever had any ill will towards me."

"That's the truth, Mr. Grimsby," replied Garboard, taking the offered hand and shaking it heartily. "I am only sorry and ashamed that I ever allowed myself to engage in my owner's dirty work. I don't excuse myself. I only ask to be forgiven this time."

"Freely I forgive you."

"Thank you, sir. I never had the least heart in the business," said the captain, as he went over the side into the boat.

I ordered one of our boats to be lowered to assist in transporting the seamen to the Hermia. I wondered that Miles did not come on deck, for I did not believe he could be asleep with so much noise as was made by the tramping feet on deck above him. He must have suspected that something was going on, and his conduct seemed very strange to me.

"Captain Farringford, we are one hand short now," said Spelter. "I like that first man we brought off from the Whitewing, the one that swung out her main boom."

"Ship him, if you can."

Spelter offered him the same wages that our crew received, and he was but too glad to accept the lay, especially as we should soon go to England. In half an hour our boat was hoisted up at the davits, and the Hermia had filled away, the crew giving us three cheers as she did so. Our vessel seemed very quiet and lonesome after the crowd had left her. I was glad to be rid of Osborne, for I did not like the looks of him. I was afraid he had a mission which he was yet to execute, and it was a relief to know that blue water rolled between him and Larry. I believed that Captain Garboard wished to be an honest man, and, away from Miles, I had no doubt he would be so.

Larry and I went into the cabin, after I had given the mate directions for the night. The door of the state-room occupied by Miles was still closed, and it was evident he had not left it since he first entered it. I had no difficulty in believing that he would be thoroughly astonished in the morning, when he discovered that all his late companions had left him.

"It looks lonely here," said Larry; "but I am not sorry to get rid of the crowd."

"Nor I. We are at home again now. Isn't it strange that Miles don't show himself? He could not have been asleep through all this excitement."

"Probably he has been. He carries an opiate in his pocket."

"What?"

"Brandy."

"Does Miles drink?"

"Only after the day is over. In the evening he boozes till it makes him sleepy. He used to get out his brandy bottle at nine o'clock, and take three or four nippers. Then he was so tight he could hardly turn in."

"I am surprised."

"I'm not; for a man that has the devil in one form is very likely to have him in half a dozen forms," added Larry.

"But you haven't told me your story yet, Larry."

"I will. Miles was very pleasant when I went on board the Whitewing off the Battery. I was in high hope that we should make an arrangement. We had a nice supper in his cabin, with wine and liquor enough on the table to float the yacht. He insisted that I should drink, begged and teased me, and finally was angry because I would not. He told me I couldn't be his friend, as I professed, if I wouldn't drink with him. A year ago it would have been the easiest thing in the world for me to do so. But I haven't tasted a drop since we met for the first time, Phil."

"Of course you didn't humor him."

"Certainly not; but he drank enough for both of us. I opened upon the question that was nearest to my heart, for my only desire was to make peace with him, not particularly because I was afraid of him, but because brethren, and even cousins, should agree, and I knew that my grandfather would be delighted to have us friends. I asked him squarely what he wanted of me, what I could do to satisfy him. He told me that nothing I could do would satisfy him, except the confession that I was an impostor, and that I had deceived Sir Philip. While I was reasoning with him on the folly of such a demand, and assuring him that I could not falsify the truth, even if I wished to do so, I heard the flapping of the mainsail on deck, and the rattling of the foreto'-bobbin forward. Just then Miles became very eloquent in the defence of his own right, and in explanation of the injury I had done him. I began to be suspicious that something was wrong, but he would not permit me to interrupt him."

"Did you know the vessel was getting under way?" I asked.

"I knew that something was going on, but I couldn't tell exactly what. You see I hadn't got the hang of the foreto'-bobbin. Miles talked so fast after he had oiled his tongue with a whole bottle of sherry, that I couldn't get a word in edgewise. Among other things, he said he was in love with Lady Somebody,— I forgot whom,— and his heart would be only a shell to her without any coronet or baronet on it. Then the yacht keeled over a little, and I began to perceive the odor of a small mouse."

"Well, what did you do?" I asked, much interested.

"I went to the cabin door and found it locked on the outside. Miles stopped talking then, and laughed. I went to the door by which the cabin steward had brought in the supper. That was locked, and Miles laughed louder than before. In a few moments I was fully satisfied that the Whitewing was under way. What could I do? That was the question I asked myself then. Of course I fully realized I was the victim of misplaced confidence. I put my hand on the revolver in my pocket but somehow I didn't feel wicked, and hadn't the slightest inclination to shoot anybody. I expected that Miles would look tragic, and do some stunning thing; but he didn't. In fact, he only laughed. When a man is good-natured, Phil, whatever he is, I don't like to be cross. I laughed, too; but Miles, who was tipsy, was rather more demonstrative than I was. He assured me it was only a practical joke, and I told him that I fully appreciated it. It was useless for me to kick, for I couldn't hit anything. I could have used up Miles in the twinkling of an eye; but I must fight the whole crew in order to accomplish anything."

"What did he intend to do with you, Larry?"

"That's more than I know."

"Didn't he threaten you, or indicate in any manner what he intended to do?"

"No; he never gave me a hint of anything. I sat down at the table with him again, and attempted to talk over our relations once more; but he was too tipsy to have an idea, and I gave it up. He pointed to a state-room on the starboard side, and wished me to make myself entirely at home, and to be as happy as I could. Presently the door of the cabin was unlocked, and the captain came down.

"'They are after us,' said he.

"'Who?' asked Miles, with a drunken start.

"'The other yacht.'

"I saw that you were not expected to follow us, and that your movements annoyed Miles and the captain very much. As the door was open, I went on deck and no one attempted to restrain me, or otherwise interfere with my movements. I saw the Blanche after us, and I assure you I began to enjoy the race, for the fact that you were following me seemed to drive from my mind any suspicion of personal peril. At one time we gained very rapidly on the Blanche."

"That was when Osborne put out the drag," I added, explaining the trick.

"If the Blanche was not expected to follow, I don't see why Osborne was sent on board of her."

"Probably to provide against emergencies," I suggested.

"You know all about the voyage as well as

I do. Miles was rather morose the next morning, for the Blanche was overhauling him very rapidly. He and the captain had a long talk, after which he seemed to feel better. I kept good-natured all the time, and made some very bad jokes. When Miles got tipsy the next night, I had a talk with Captain Garboard, and tried to find out what they intended to do with me. I did not succeed. I began to be a little impatient under this kind of a life, and I made up my mind that when the Blanche again came as near the Whitewing as she had several times, I would jump overboard, and let you pick me up. I put a piece of plank in a convenient place to use in the water. You came quite near, and I was on the point of leaping into the sea with my plank, when Captain Garboard laid his flat paw on my shoulder. He assured me I should certainly be drowned, and that he had seen the fin of a big shark that morning. I don't think he would have interfered if he had not been afraid I should be drowned or gnawed by a shark. I gave it up, and went below. After dinner I went into my state-room to take a nap. When I awoke, the door was locked. Of course the captain had told

Miles what I was about; but I am sure if my amiable cousin had known there was a man-eater astern, he would have permitted me to jump overboard. My meals were handed in to me by the steward, and I spent two days reading the Bible, as I told you. You know the rest."

We discussed the matter for an hour, and then turned in, Larry occupying a berth in the cabin.

CHAPTER XI.

IN WHICH PHIL AND LARRY MAKE SOME NEW ACQUAINTANCES AT ST. GEORGE.

WHEN I went on deck in the morning, at rather a late hour, the Blanche was off the principal entrance to the harbor of St. George, with a signal flying for a pilot. The wind had subsided to a gentle breeze from the westward. We had been in the circles of one of the revolving storms which prevail in the region, and the Hermia had probably experienced its full violence. But the weather was beautiful now, and the bright sun seemed to be an earnest of the clearer future before us, now that Miles had apparently been deprived of his power to injure Larry. We took a pilot in a short time, and, though the wind was not fair, we got into the harbor and anchored before Larry turned out. The paying out of the cable waked him, and he thrust his head out of the curtains.

"How's this, Phil? Has the foreto'-bobbin broke down?" he asked, evidently startled by the noise of the rattling chain.

"The foreto'-bobbin's all right, and we have come to anchor in the harbor of St. George."

"Have you seen the dragon?"

"No. He was up late last night, and hasn't turned out yet. But we are right under the lee of Cherrystone Hill."

"St. George is nobody without the dragon," replied Larry, as he proceeded to dress himself. "Is Miles stirring yet?"

"I haven't heard from him since he turned in last night."

"That's twelve hours ago. Perhaps he is sick, or something has happened to him," suggested my friend, with a troubled look. "He couldn't sleep twelve hours on a stretch."

I went to the door of the state-room and knocked. Miles promptly answered, and we were assured that he was still alive. I told him it was eight o'clock, and that we were at anchor in port. Presently he came out of the room, with his overcoat on his arm."

"Good morning, Miles," said Larry.

"Good morning," replied he, coldly, as he looked about the cabin, as if in search of some one. "Is Captain Garboard here?"

"He is not," I answered. "Captain Garboard left the Blanche last night, and is now on his voyage to England."

Miles looked at me in utter astonishment; and I related to him all the circumstances of the departure of the Whitewing's people. He appeared to be very much disconcerted, and disposed to be angry.

"Didn't you hear any noise last night?" I asked.

"I did not," he replied.

"I supposed you must be awake, for the men were tramping on the deck over your head for an hour."

"I heard nothing. I am a heavy sleeper at sea. Why was I not called?"

"We spoke to Captain Garboard about seeing you, but he declined to disturb you."

"The villain! Have all the crew of the Whitewing gone?"

"Every one of them, including Osborne. As they had lost their voyage, they were anxious to get home."

"I am anxious to get home also, and they ought to have called me. Fitzgerald would have given me a passage."

"Don't trouble yourself about that, Miles," interposed his cousin. "I will give you a passage, and place my yacht at your disposal."

Miles's face flushed, and he did not even thank Larry for the courteous offer.

"Breakfast is all ready, Mr. Grimsby," I continued. "Take a seat, sir."

"I will not impose myself upon your hospitality any longer than is necessary," he answered, very stiffly; and I could not help feeling that we were heaping coals of fire upon his head.

"Of course you are free to go or stay, as you please, Miles," said Larry, gently; "but my vessel and all that I have are at your disposal. Whatever wrong you have done me, whatever wrong you have intended to do me, I shall forgive and forget, whether you go or stay."

"I am not to be caught by any such cant as that," replied Miles, sourly.

"I am sincere in all I say," added Larry. "I hope you will breakfast with me, or at least at my table; for if my presence is disagreeable to you I will retire."

"We can never be friends," said Miles, stalking across the cabin to the steps. "You can neither coax nor drive me from my position."

He went on deck, and I followed him. Hailing a negro in a shore boat, he left the yacht without saying good by, or thanking us for the trouble we had taken to save him from his fate on the rocks.

"It's no use, Phil," said Larry, shaking his head. "I have forgiven him in my heart, but his teeth are set against me."

"Your conscience is clear, whatever he may do. He evidently regards your course as an attempt to coax him into an agreement."

"I don't want to quarrel with him."

We sat down to breakfast, and continued to consider the question; but there seemed to be no way to make peace between the cousins.

"Boat with two ladies coming alongside, sir," said Mr. Spelter, at the companion-way.

"Ladies!" exclaimed Larry, leaving the table and going on deck, though not till we had finished the meal.

"Is Mr. Grimsby on board?" I heard some one ask in the boat.

"He is, sir."

In the stern-sheets of the boat were two ladies and a gentleman, whom the mate invited to come on board. The accommodation steps were already in place, and the party were assisted to the deck. The gentleman had asked if Mr. Grimsby was on board, and I wondered who in this place could know Larry. One of the ladies was young and very pretty—this was the first observation I made. The other lady and the gentleman were elderly people.

"Ah, Mr. Grimsby, I am very glad indeed to see you!" exclaimed the young lady, as Larry presented himself on the quarter-deck, extending her hand to him.

"I thank you; and I assure you I am equally happy to see you," replied Larry, taking the offered hand. "But I fear —"

"I am so glad you are safe," interposed the lady. "We heard that a vessel was wrecked yesterday, and we feared it was your yacht."

"Fortunately it was not mine," added Larry, with admirable self-possession.

"And what a beautiful yacht she is!" exclaimed the fair lady, glancing around her at the well-ordered deck and rigging. "You can't tell how glad I am that you have come, for I am terribly weary of this dull place. I would rather die in England than live here."

"You don't mean that, Lady Eleanor," interposed the elderly lady.

"Yes, I do mean it, aunt. It is the stupidest place in the world, if it is summer all winter. When shall you be ready to sail for England, Mr. Grimsby."

"In a few days," answered Larry.

"The sooner the better. But do let me see the yacht. May I go down into the cabin?"

"Certainly, Lady Eleanor; the yacht is entirely at your service. But —"

"It is very kind of you to offer us a passage to England, Mr. Grimsby," rattled the lady. "But how is your grandfather, Sir Philip? It was very stupid in me not to inquire before."

"He was quite well the last time I heard from him," replied Larry, as he conducted the lady to the cabin.

"Why, it's a little palace!" exclaimed Lady Eleanor.

"It is a very comfortable cabin."

"It is more than that. It is elegant. I'm sure we shall be very happy here, aunt."

"Certainly we ought to be," replied the elderly lady.

"Pray be seated, ladies," said Larry.

"May I look into this state-room?" asked Lady Eleanor.

"Excuse me, but I prefer that you should not until it is put in order."

The young lady took the seat which Larry offered her, and continued to gaze about the cabin for a moment. Then she looked earnestly at my friend.

"Dear me, Mr. Grimsby! I think you look ever so much better than you did when I saw you last," she added.

"When was that?" asked he, quietly.

"Don't you remember it?"

"I really do not."

"Why, Mr. Grimsby, what a wicked memory yours must be!"

"Really, Lady Eleanor, I don't think I ever saw you before in my life."

"Never saw me!"

"I think you have made a mistake," laughed Larry.

"Are you not Mr. Grimsby?"

"I am; but not the Mr. Grimsby for whom you take me. I am Lawrence Grimsby, not Miles."

The lady blushed deeply, and was very much disturbed. The other visitors also were much surprised.

"Why, you look just like him!" exclaimed Lady Eleanor, when she in a measure recovered from her confusion.

"But I look better than he did when you saw him last," added Larry, wickedly. "I fear Miles will not consider that a compliment, though I do."

"I haven't seen Mr. Miles for more than a year; but you are the very image of him."

"I have been taken for him before. He is my cousin."

"I was not aware that he had a cousin before," said the gentleman.

Larry told the strange story of his father, and of his own return to Grimsby Hall, which was as yet known to but few persons in England.

"But Mr. Miles wrote to me that he should come to the Bermudas in April or May, and offered us all a passage home in his yacht."

"His yacht was wrecked yesterday; but all

hands were saved, and Miles landed half an hour before you came on board."

"Then we are not to go to England in Mr. Miles's yacht, after all," sighed Lady Eleanor, with an expression of intense disappointment on her face.

"That will be quite impossible, for the Whitewing has gone to pieces on the reef."

"I anticipated a great deal of pleasure from the voyage in a yacht; and now I must go home some other way."

"Permit me to place my state-room at your disposal, Lady Eleanor," added Larry, very politely. "We are going to England, and should be delighted with your company and that of your friends."

"You are too kind," exclaimed the beautiful young lady, her face lighting up with pleasure.

"But we could not think of trespassing upon your hospitality to that extent," interposed Mr. Langford, the elderly gentleman.

"It will be no trespass, for I assure you I shall consider myself the obliged party. Certainly nothing could be more agreeable to me than such delightful company."

"I thank you with all my heart, Mr. Grimsby;

and unless my friends object, I shall accept the invitation."

"We are certainly very much indebted to you, sir," added Mr. Langford. "Your polite offer places us under very great obligations to you. Lady Eleanor had set her heart upon going home in a yacht. But perhaps we had better consult the governor, who is the lady's uncle, before we give you a final answer. I fear we shall annoy you too much."

"Not at all. I only regret that I can offer you but one state-room," said Larry.

"Yes, you can; you can offer mine," I interposed, for I could not think of occupying my room while the owner of the Blanche had only a berth in the cabin.

"Good, Phil! Then we can accommodate you all very comfortably."

"But we cannot think of depriving you of your rooms," protested the gentleman; and both the ladies joined in the protest.

"We shall be very well berthed in the cabin," replied Larry, as he opened the door of his state-room, which had just been put in order by the steward.

"How elegant! It's a little *boudoir!*" exclaimed Lady Eleanor, clapping her hands with delight as she entered the room.

We went over the yacht with our new friends, who expressed their satisfaction in the warmest terms. They soon took leave of us; but I had ordered a boat to be lowered, and Larry and I reached the landing-place almost as soon as they did. Mr. Langford invited us to visit the residence of the governor, which we did, and were duly presented to this distinguished functionary. He gave us a very pleasant reception, and asked us to dinner that day. We promised to come, and then took a tramp to the farthest end of the island.

"Phil, I've just got it through my thick head," said my friend, when we had left the governor's, "and I don't know but I have made a mess of it."

"What do you mean?"

"It seems that Miles came here for a purpose. This pretty Lady Eleanor is the lady he wishes to marry, and he came down here to see her and convey her home in his yacht; and I have invited her to go to England with me!"

"I don't see that any harm has been done."

"The idea of my sailing this lady home, and leaving Miles here, is slightly odd."

"You offered Miles a passage, and he declined the offer."

"He will be the maddest man in the Bermuda Islands if the lady and her friends should conclude to accept the invitation."

"They will accept it, you may depend. When a pretty girl, like her ladyship, makes up her mind to do anything, she generally carries the day. She wants to go home in a yacht, and she will go."

"Miles may persuade her not to do so."

"Miles has not logic or rhetoric enough to do anything of the kind."

At noon we went on board of the Blanche and lunched. We dressed for dinner, and went on shore in the middle of the afternoon. At the landing-place we encountered Miles, who had evidently been waiting there for us. I concluded that he had seen Lady Eleanor, and that there was a tempest gathering, which was now to burst upon the head of my friend.

"Lawrence," said Miles, as we landed, "it is very hard for me to ask a favor of you."

"I am sorry it is so hard; but it is not my fault, you know," replied Larry. "Anything in reason that you can ask of me I will grant."

"Thank you. How much did your yacht cost you?"

"About three thousand pounds."

"I wish to purchase her, and will give you six thousand pounds for her," continued Miles, with some hesitation and embarrassment.

"I do not wish to sell her," replied Larry, astonished at the proposition. "I have had her fitted up to suit me, and all my plans for the summer depend upon her."

"I did not suppose you wished to sell her, and therefore I asked you to do so as a favor to me. Long before I left home I wrote to some friends here, informing them that I should visit the Bermudas in April or May, and inviting them to take passage to England in my yacht. The loss of the Whitewing places me in a very awkward position, from which you alone have the power to relieve me."

"I understand you, and will consider your proposition," replied Larry.

"I will employ all your crew, with one exception, and carry out all your engagements with them."

"You shall have my answer to-morrow;" and Miles left us.

"If that isn't cheek, I don't know what cheek is," I added, as we walked towards the governor's.

CHAPTER XII.

IN WHICH PHIL AND LARRY DINE AT THE GOVERNOR'S, AND A QUARREL ENSUES.

LARRY seemed to be in deep thought as we walked up the street, and I did not disturb him. I was very curious to know what action he intended to take upon the astounding proposition of his villanous cousin. Since his escape from the Whitewing he had talked a great deal of the truths he had learned in his two days' study of the Bible. But I was afraid he was mistaken in his Christian duty, which certainly did not require him wholly to sacrifice himself to the pleasure of one who sought only to injure him. The large sum of money which Miles offered for the Blanche had no influence whatever upon the mind of Larry, and I knew that he would not accept any more than the fair value of the vessel, if he sold her.

"What do you think of that offer, Phil?" asked Larry, after we had walked some distance.

"I don't know that I ought to say what I think," I replied. "I do not wish to influence you in a matter between you and your cousin."

"Do you think I ought to accept the offer?"

"I think you had better settle that question yourself, Larry."

"Don't desert me, Phil."

"I will not; but the case is a family matter."

"If I could have peace with Miles, I would make him a present of the Blanche," said Larry, very much perplexed. "He has come down from his high horse far enough to ask a favor of me, for of course the sale of the vessel is all nonsense. It doesn't make a bit of difference with me whether I have three thousand pounds more or less; but if I can make an arrangement with him whereby we can be friends, or at least dwell together upon the earth in peace, I shall be satisfied to sacrifice my own pleasure, and yours, too, for that matter, Phil, for we are to spend the season together, and we have laid out a very enjoyable trip."

"Never mind me."

"I will not, if I can heal the breach, Phil; but I shall be grateful to you for not interfering."

We reached the governor's temporary residence, for his capital was at Hamilton, on another island. We found Miles there, as we expected. He had seen Lady Eleanor and her friends, and had been apprised of the invitation the party had received to go to England in the Blanche. His plan to buy the yacht was doubtless an expedient to deprive us of our interesting passenger. As the ladies had not yet appeared, we had an opportunity to consider the proposition still further.

"I have been thinking of your offer, Miles," said Larry, seating himself by the side of his cousin. "I understand and appreciate the motives which induce you to make it. You know that the most earnest desire of my life is to have peace and happiness in our family."

"What do you mean by 'our family'?" demanded Miles, haughtily.

"I mean Sir Philip Grimsby and his grandsons, as well as all others connected with him or them."

"Go on," added Miles, with a palpable sneer on his face, which was not hopeful for a favorable result.

"I am confident that Sir Philip will treat us both alike. If you will sign a paper acknowledging my rights, agreeing to live at peace with me —"

"I will not," said he, vehemently.

"I ask it of you as a favor, that you will simply acknowledge what has been established to the satisfaction of Sir Philip and his legal advisers, and be at peace with me."

"I regard you as an impostor," growled Miles; "and I cannot be on friendly terms with such a person."

"Then, without waiting for to-morrow, a decent self-respect compels me to decline your proposition in regard to the Blanche," answered Larry, very mildly and gently. "At the same time, if the Lady Eleanor and her friends conclude to accept the invitation I have given them to return to England in the Blanche, I will place a berth in the cabin — the best I can offer you — at your disposal."

"You know very well that I shall refuse such an offer. Nothing can induce me to place myself under the slightest obligation to you," answered Miles, stiffly and proudly.

"I think that the obligation—if such you choose to regard it—of giving you a berth in my cabin is vastly less than that of giving up the yacht entirely to you, and setting aside all my plans for the season. But you have a right to your own opinion."

The question was settled; and the ladies presently entered the drawing-room.

Lady Eleanor was certainly lovely. She was not more than seventeen, and a perpetual smile played upon her pretty lips. I could not blame Miles for loving her, and I could not wonder that he was willing to sacrifice his pride so far, for her sake, as to ask my friend for his yacht. After observing them for half an hour, I concluded that the lady was not in love with Miles, if he was with her; indeed, I thought she avoided him to some extent, and she certainly talked more with Larry than with him. Agreeably to the English custom, the ladies retired after coffee, and the gentlemen sipped their wine and engaged in conversation. Larry and I, as usual, drank nothing stronger than coffee; but I noticed that Miles, doubtless preyed upon by his disappointment, punished his bottle very severely. If he had been happy his wine would have made him happier; as he was ugly, it made him uglier.

The governor asked me something about my friend's relations to Sir Philip, and I told him enough of the story to enable him to understand them. He was very much interested, and listened to the narrative, at one end of the table, while Miles and a government official were pushing the bottle at the other. I spoke in a low tone, but somehow Miles overheard me, or suspected what I was talking about. He rose from his seat, and walked rather unsteadily to our end of the table. I suspended my narrative, for I had given all the material portions of it.

"You are speaking of Lawrence Grimsby. He is an impostor and a swindler," roared Miles, savagely.

"You forget, Mr. Grimsby, that you are in the presence of gentlemen," interposed the governor, sternly, as he rose from his chair and held up his hand with a deprecatory gesture.

"I beg your pardon, governor, for saying it before you and your friends; but it is the truth," replied Miles, more mildly. "If he had the instincts of a gentleman, he would resent it."

"Nothing which a tipsy man can say affects me," laughed Larry.

"Do you mean to insult me?" demanded Miles, shaking his fist in his cousin's face.

"Mr. Grimsby, take your seat!" said the governor, angrily. "You insult me by such conduct in my presence."

"Let my wrongs be my apology," replied Miles, awed and abashed by the words of his host, as he dropped into a chair.

"This is not a question for me to settle," added the governor; "and I will not tolerate a quarrel in my presence."

"I beg your excellency's pardon," stammered Miles. "My wrongs for a moment caused me to forget myself."

"You should apologize to Mr. Lawrence Grimsby, whom you assailed with the most opprobrious epithets."

"I cannot do that, even to retain your excellency's esteem."

"I do not require it," interposed Larry.

"But I do. A quarrel commenced at my table must be ended there," stormed the choleric governor.

"I can apologize to your excellency, but not to one whom I justly and properly stigmatized, though the time and place were badly chosen."

"I beg you will not insist upon any further apology," said Larry,

"If I do not, I trust that Mr. Lawrence's magnanimity will be fully appreciated," added the governor.

"Since I have been assailed here, and stigmatized as an impostor and a swindler, it is but just that my defence should be heard," continued Larry, pleasantly; for he kept his temper remarkably well under the savage provocation to which he was subjected. "May I ask your excellency to read two or three letters to me from Sir Philip Grimsby."

My friend produced his letters; the governor and Mr. Langford read them attentively. Both of them knew Sir Philip intimately, and they left no doubt whatever in their minds in regard to Larry's position.

"I am entirely satisfied, Mr. Grimsby," said the governor. "If I had any doubts before, I have none now. My niece is very anxious to accept your kind invitation to return to England in your yacht, and in her behalf I accept it. Of course she will be attended by Mr. and Mrs. Langford."

"Certainly, sir. The invitation was extended to them, and to Mr. Miles also," answered Larry.

This was enough to complete the disgust of Miles, for the governor had spoken loud enough for him to hear, and he soon after retired. The conversation was continued for an hour longer by those who remained. I deemed it my duty, in a quiet way, to introduce the fact that Larry was already engaged to a lady in New York, so that the friends of our fair passenger might not suppose that the gallant owner of the Blanche intended to win a titled wife by his courtesy. We spent a very pleasant evening with the party in the drawing-room, and Lady Eleanor was delighted when told she was to make the voyage in the yacht. At ten o'clock we retired, and went on board of the Blanche. We had a long talk about the events of the evening; but not a particle of progress had been made towards a reconciliation with Miles; indeed, such a happy event seemed more distant than ever.

The climate of the Bermudas at this season was delicious. It was neither hot nor cold, and everything was in bloom. Larry and I enjoyed the air and the scenery. The next morning we took another long tramp on shore, visiting some arrow-root and other farms where vegetables were raised for the New York market. We were much interested in the excursion, and we agreed that a tramp on foot affords the best facilities for seeing the people and the manners and customs of any country. We arranged several tramps in Europe; and I think if we had taken them all, they would have occupied half a dozen seasons.

As we were entering the town of St. George, which contains about five hundred houses, on our return, we saw a singular-looking being approaching us. He was a man at least six and a half feet high, very gaunt and thin. His pants were tight, and he wore the shortest of frock coats, whose skirts hardly covered his hips. Both of these garments were of dark green, and the coat was buttoned to his chin. On his head was a cap of the same color, with no visor, tipped very far over on one side. His only beard was a tremendous heavy mustache, which was red enough to light a match. His hair was bushy, and of the same color. He looked like an exaggeration of some of the British army swells, — privates and non-commissioned officers, — whom I had seen in London and other English cities; yet the absence of certain distinguishing marks assured me that he did not belong to the army. He was a person who might have been thirty-five, or forty-five. I could not form an opinion in regard to his age. His nose was very red, and his face flushed; in fact, he had raised a very abundant crop of toddy-blossoms. Larry and I could not help staring at this long, spindling specimen of humanity; and I confess that our risibles were so rudely exercised by his singular appearance that we found it rather difficult to preserve a decorous gravity.

"Good morning, gentlemen," said the lofty stranger, raising his little cap, and bowing with the most exuberant politeness. "Have I the honor to address Mr. Lawrence Grimsby and Captain Farringford, of the magnificent yacht which is at anchor in the harbor?"

"Undoubtedly you have, sir," replied Larry, lightly. "May I ask whom I have the honor of addressing?"

"Certainly, sir. Allow me to introduce myself as Captain Gregory McFordingham, formerly in the service of the Honorable East India Company, but now detached and unemployed."

"Happy to make your acquaintance, Captain McFordingham; and I hope we shall not quarrel," added Larry.

"Quarrel! What could have suggested such a thought to you?" exclaimed he, with a dramatic start. "Has any reckless vandal been taking liberties with my reputation?"

"Not that I am aware of, Captain McFordingham, for I assure you this is the first time I have had the honor to see or hear of you."

"Is it possible? And yet we ought to know each other better. I imagine that I am addressing my conversation at this particular moment to Mr. Grimsby, and not to the gallant Captain Farringford."

"Your brilliant imagination does not mislead you," laughed Larry, who enjoyed the tall gentleman exceedingly.

"I thought so; but no offence to you, Captain Farringford," continued our new acquaintance, touching his miniature cap and bowing to me. "I am fully informed in regard to the captain's gallant conduct in the rescue of the officers and crew of the vessel that was unhappily wrecked near Mill's Breaker the other day. Permit me to add, Captain Farringford, that I admire and applaud your noble gallantry and your magnanimous self-sacrifice."

"May I ask to whom I am indebted for this generous setting forth of my conduct, which certainly does not warrant such extravagant praise?" I asked.

"Ah, captain, true bravery is always modest, and you will permit me to say that you are not the best and truest exponent of your own noble deeds."

"But will you tell me who said anything to you about me and my conduct?"

"My excellent friend, the governor of the Bermudas, who is always among the first to exalt and magnify a noble and generous act."

Perhaps I was too suspicious, but I was afraid the fellow was an agent of Miles Grimsby. However, the governor knew the whole story of the shipwreck, and his information seemed to have been properly obtained.

"I was about to say that we ought to know each other better, Mr. Grimsby, when the natural modesty of Captain Farringford diverted the conversation," continued Captain McFordingham.

"Undoubtedly we ought; and as we have been remiss in this respect in the past, we must make amends for it in the future," replied Larry.

"Quite right, Mr. Grimsby; and, beyond the demands of friendship and good fellowship, I must offer the additional inducement of a relationship between us, for sir Phillip Grimsby, your grandfather, — the noblest and wealthiest baronet in all England, let me add, in parenthesis, — married a McFordingham, as you are doubtless aware."

Larry confessed that he had not studied the genealogy of his family enough to be aware of the fact.

"Well, sir, the deceased and lamented wife of Sir Phillip had a brother, whose grandson I have the honor to be. But I have particular business with you, gentlemen; and will you accept the hospitality of my poor lodgings for half an hour?"

My friend enjoyed the adventure too much to allow it to be broken off thus prematurely, and we accompanied Captain McFordingham to a tap-room connected with a lodging-house.

CHAPTER XIII.

IN WHICH PHIL AND LARRY DECLINE VARIOUS OFFERS.

CAPTAIN GREGORY McFORDINGHAM doubled up his length of six and one half feet in a chair, and invited us to be seated. I could not exactly understand why we were in such a place, and with such a man, for I need not say that I had no respect for our magnificent and over-courteous host. The only explanation I could make to myself of our position was, that my friend had a keen appreciation of the humor of the fellow, who, however, did not seem to be aware that he was amusing us.

"Brandy and water for me," said the captain, as a waiter presented himself at the table. "Gentlemen, will you have wine, ale, or spirits? For my part, I always take brandy in this climate; it agrees with me best. But don't let me influence you. Shall it be brandy?"

"Thank you, Captain McFordingham; but speaking for myself and my accomplished nautical friend, we don't drink brandy," replied Larry.

"Ah, I forgot. Whiskey is the national beverage of America.—Waiter, let it be whiskey," added our long host.

"Whiskey may be the national beverage of America; but we do not use it."

"No? Shall it be gin?"

"It shall not. We never drink liquor of any kind."

"Many people do not; though I confess that the fact is a paradox to me. In my estimation, good French brandy is the most wholesome drink a person can take, especially in this climate. But of course I respect your judgment."

"Thank you. You are very considerate, and even magnanimous. But in regard to brandy, I disagree with you utterly," replied Larry.

"I cannot speak with authority in regard to the wines of this place, for I never drink them, preferring brandy, as I said. But I dare say they have good sherry."

"As good as any in the United Kingdom," interposed the waiter.

"I dare say it is good enough; but we don't drink sherry," laughed Larry.

"Ah, Madeira.—How is your Madeira, waiter?"

"Excellent, sir; better nor it is in England, Captain O'Crackbone says so; which he ought to know, sir."

"Excuse us, sir; but we don't drink Madeira. We heard of a man who was poisoned by drinking it."

"Bless my 'eart! Not with our Madeira, sir!" exclaimed the waiter, with horror.

"I can't say it was yours; but we never touch any Madeira," answered Larry, shaking his head.

"Then let it be Port. Have you any real Port, waiter — not the decoction of logwood?"

"Our Port comes to us direct from 'Porto, which it is good from nowhere else, sir, you know."

"We don't drink Port, captain. In fact, we don't drink wine at all, sir."

"Is it possible?" ejaculated our tall host, with an expression of pity on his face. "They have the best of English ales here."

"Yes, sir; Hinglish hale in its purity," added the waiter, with enthusiasm.

"Alsop, Bass, Falkirk. Let me recommend Falkirk."

"I think we will not drink any Falkirk."

"Alsop's very good," said the captain. "I used to drink Alsop myself, once. But what is the use of wasting one's time over half a dozen glasses of ale, when one of brandy will produce the same effect? Waiter, bring Alsop."

"I beg your pardon, Captain McFordingham, but I believe I neglected to say that we don't drink Alsop."

"Then Bass. Some people prefer Bass."

"Doubtless they do; but we do not," added Larry; "it is rather heady."

"What else have you, waiter?" asked our host, who evidently regarded his guests as altogether too fastidious.

"I think we 'ave named everything we 'as, sir, which it is the best to be 'ad anywhere."

"I don't like to be too abrupt in these little social interchanges; but perhaps it is now time for me to say that we don't drink anything," continued Larry, with becoming gravity.

"Don't drink anything!" exclaimed Captain McFordingham, springing to his feet, and elevating his entire length before us. "Is it possible?"

"My amiable marine friend here never tasted liquor, wine, or beer in his life," added Larry, pointing to me. "A year ago I concluded to follow his illustrious example."

"Is it possible that you are teetotalers?"

"We are."

"I've heard of such, but I never saw one before," said our host, with an expression of amazement, as he dropped into his chair again. "Of course I can't drink brandy and water alone."

"I really can't advise you to do so," responded Larry. "I think you observed that you had business with us."

"I did, and you were kind enough to come here with me. With your permission, I will proceed to open my business. — Nothing, waiter," he added, with dignity, to the man who was waiting for his order. "I never drink alone in presence of company."

"We have some Rochelle brandy, which it is very good, sir."

"None," added the captain, waving his hand at the waiter, who retired.

At that moment Miles Grimsby entered the tap-room from an inner apartment, and I concluded that his lodgings were in the house. I saw that he gave a start when he perceived us; and he then walked to the table, where we sat.

"I beg your pardon, gentlemen," said he, lifting his Scotch cap. "The Unicorn is coming into the harbor at this moment—"

"Is it possible?" exclaimed Captain McFordingham, who seemed to have no acquaintance with Miles.

"I saw her from my window up stairs. I do not know how long she will remain; but I wish to speak a word to you, Mr. Grimsby, as soon as possible, for I shall go to New York in her, and thence to England, unless some different arrangement should be made."

"Then, if you please, gentlemen, will you excuse me for half an hour?" interposed our tall friend. "If the steamer is coming in, I have a bit of business to do."

"If we are not here when you return, you will find us on board of the Blanche," replied Larry; and the tall captain bowed himself off.

Miles Grimsby took the chair he had vacated, and the waiter immediately presented himself.

"A bottle of sherry," said Miles.

"Sherry, sir, which it is very good sherry we 'ave, too, sir," answered the man, who was so fluent in recommending the merchandise of the house that he might have been supposed to share its profits.

As Larry was not Miles's keeper, however much he needed one, my friend did not interfere with the order. The waiter brought three glasses and set them before us. Although Larry and I protested, the man filled ours.

"I hardly expect you to drink wine with me," said Miles.

"You are aware that we don't drink wine with any one, even at the risk of being regarded as prigs," answered Larry.

"We need not discuss that question. Have you finally decided in regard to the yacht, Lawrence?"

"I have. I cannot accept your liberal offer, Miles. But a berth in the cabin is at your disposal," answered Larry. "As you are doubtless aware, Lady Eleanor and her friends have concluded to take passage in the Blanche."

"I am aware of it," replied Miles, draining his glass; "and your mention of the fact is the greatest insult you can cast upon me," he added, bringing his fist down upon the table with a force that slopped half the wine out of the glasses before us.

"I did not intend it as an insult; and, if you regard it as such, I tender my apology," said Larry, mildly.

"Not content with robbing me of my fortune and my title, you seek to turn the Lady Eleanor against me," raved Miles.

"Indeed, I seek nothing of the kind."

"When I called upon her this morning, she declined to see me," said Miles, savagely. "Yesterday she received me with the utmost kindness; to-day she discards me. I owe all this to you."

"If you will excuse me, I think you owe it to yourself."

"Don't taunt me. You have done your worst already. You have invited the Lady Eleanor to go to England in your yacht. You have seen her; you know her. Shall I not hear, when I reach England, that she is engaged to you?"

"No!" exclaimed Larry, vehemently. "Or, if you do, contradict it on the instant; for it will not be true. You know that I am engaged to Blanche Fennimore."

"Blanche Fennimore!" sneered Miles; "what is she but a beggar?"

"That does not alter the case."

"Lady Eleanor is young, beautiful, and the daughter of an earl. She consents to take passage in your yacht to England. Am I fool enough to suppose you would not discard Blanche Fennimore for such a prize as Lady Eleanor?"

"Most certainly I would not discard her for a countess, a duchess, or even a princess."

"You may think so now; but I know the world better," growled Miles. "Then you used every effort yesterday, at dinner, to prejudice the people there against me."

"You should not charge me with the consequences of your own action, Miles. I am willing to forgive and forget the wrong you have done me."

"Are you, indeed?" sneered Miles.

"When you charged me with being an impostor, yesterday, I only defended myself. I could do no less. And I think I proved all I said by Sir Philip's letters. Your plans have miscarried; but you should blame yourself not me. You lost your yacht in an attempt to kidnap me, and dispose of me, in what manner I know not. If you have lost the Lady Eleanor, it is the result of your own misconduct. I have offered to compromise with you, and you refuse. I can do no more."

"Give me no more of your cant. You will not sell your yacht for double her value?"

"I will not. But I will give you a berth in her, so that you may be with Lady Eleanor during the voyage to England."

"You know that I will not go in the same vessel with you. I must go to New York in the Unicorn."

"I have offered the best I can," added Larry.

Miles abused him for some time longer; but my friend was patient and mild, and not once did he exhibit any anger. He was very firm in the maintenance of his own rights, but willing to sacrifice a great deal, even for one who had used him so meanly. His conduct seemed to be the direct fruit of his two days' study of the Bible, of which he had spoken so enthusiastically to me. Suddenly Miles rose and left the house.

"Can I do any different, Phil?" he asked, as his cousin departed.

"No. I think you have done all that a Christian

can do. You are willing to forgive him, and to do all you can for him, even at great sacrifice to yourself," I replied.

"I am happy to find you still here," said Captain McFordingham, returning at this moment. "The steamer has to wait for the tide, and will not come in for an hour. Ah, gentlemen!"

The tall captain suddenly gave a tragic start, and looked very savage, as he regarded the half-filled wine-glasses before us.

"I beg your pardon, gentlemen; but I do not wish to consider myself insulted," continued he. "You decline to drink with me, but with another more favored individual you waive all scruples. I fought a duel in India with an officer who refused to drink with me under circumstances less glaring than the present."

"Perhaps I shall enable you to spare some of your valuable breath if I say that we have not drank; that we declined to drink with this gentleman, as we did with you," added Larry, rather impatiently, for Captain McFordingham's humor was becoming rather stupid.

"Pardon me, sir; but your glasses are half emptied," said the captain.

"What isn't in them now is on the table. But, excuse me, I think you said you had business with us."

"A gentleman drinks with a gentleman, and only with a gentleman. To refuse to drink with a gentleman is equivalent to telling him that he is no gentleman. You declined to drink with me, on the plea that you were both teetotalers; and I accepted the plea, refraining from drinking myself. I find that you took wine with another, in form if not in substance. Am I to understand that you consider me no gentleman?" demanded Captain McFordingham, with a lowering brow.

"Certainly you are to understand nothing of the sort," replied Larry, rather impatiently.

"And you, sir?" added the captain, turning to me.

"Certainly not," I answered.

"Not a gentleman?"

"You are not to understand that I consider you no gentleman. I express no opinion whatever on that subject," I added.

"Then we will reserve the whole question for another occasion," said the captain, pompously.

"I have the honor to be a purveyor of provisions, vegetables, and fruits; and I offer my services in supplying your yacht with any of these articles you may desire, in large or in small quantities."

I looked at Captain Gregory McFordingham after this communication, and I could hardly refrain from laughing in his face. The important business introduced with such a flourish, was the sale of a barrel or two of potatoes, a box of oranges, and a few cabbages.

"If this is your business, I must refer you to Captain Farringford," laughed Larry.

The tall gentleman looked at me.

"And, in turn, I must refer you to the steward of the yacht," I added.

"I always prefer to deal directly with principals," said the purveyor of cabbages.

"In this instance the steward is the principal," I replied. "If he wants any cabbages or turnips, he has the commercial cunning to enable him to purchase them."

"I shall take the liberty to call upon him immediately."

"If you have no further business with us, I

shall beg the privilege of saying good morning," said Larry.

"I beg your pardon; but I have another matter in my mind. I wish to return to England. The business of purveying is not as profitable here as I had been led to suppose, and I purpose to abandon the islands. I concluded that when my desire became known to you, it would procure me an invitation to take passage in your yacht."

"My dear Captain McFordingham, we haven't a berth in the Blanche which is long enough for you," protested Larry; "and I trust that this fact will be deemed a sufficient excuse for not inviting you."

"Perhaps you misunderstand me. I am aware that your cabin is already full; and I shall be quite content with a place in the steerage, in the forecastle, or on the kitchen floor," added the purveyor.

"My dear sir, I could not think of inviting a person of your distinguished character to take a long voyage with me, without being able to give him suitable accommodations. I fear we must decline the honor of your company," continued Larry, with great good-nature, as we moved towards the door of the tap-room.

"Mr. Grimsby, this is the third time you have insulted me to-day, and I demand satisfaction," said Captain McFordingham, savagely.

"Good morning, sir," said Larry, as we walked out into the street.

13

CHAPTER XIV.

IN WHICH PHIL AND LARRY TAKE ANOTHER TRAMP, AND AN AFFAIR OF HONOR IMPENDS.

"STOP a moment, Mr. Grimsby. The wounded honor of a gentleman is not to be healed so easily," said Captain McFordingham, placing his hand upon the shoulder of my friend.

"I am not aware, sir, that I have wounded your honor in any manner," replied Larry.

"Three times you have intimated that I am no gentleman; an insult, sir, to which I cannot submit."

"I assure you I had no intention of insulting you, and am not yet aware that I have done so. If I have, I beg your pardon. Good morning."

We walked towards the landing-place, where our boat was waiting for us; but we were closely followed by the captain, who, it seemed plain enough, was intent on picking a quarrel. We stepped into the boat, and were pulled to the Blanche.

"That fellow is determined to get up a quarrel," said Larry.

"He hasn't succeeded so far."

"And he will not. He amused me prodigiously at first. One would suppose from his manner that he was a member of the royal family. I don't think I should care to quarrel with him — he is too tall."

"He is a bully, too, and doubtless a coward also."

During our absence the Blanche had been dressed with the colors of all nations, and presented a very striking appearance. Larry had invited the governor, Lady Eleanor, Mr. and Mrs. Langford, and others, to dine on board that afternoon, and we found the preparations in a very forward state. At four o'clock the party came off, and we entertained them in princely style. Miles had been invited, in spite of his bad conduct; but, true to his malicious nature, not even the attractions of Lady Eleanor's presence could induce him to come; though, I think, no one mourned his absence. The steamer had come into the harbor, and was to sail the next day at noon, when the tide turned. We had decided to get under way at the same time, after ascertaining that our passengers would be ready.

The next morning Larry and I made another tramp on the island, for we enjoyed these walks, and the delicious air, very much. We went as far as the Martello Tower, at the western extremity of St. George, and on our return ascended Cherrystone Hill. On a cliff below we seated ourselves, to rest after the fatigues of the morning, for we had yet a couple of hours to spare. The place we had chosen was a retired spot, but so pleasant that we wished our departure was to be delayed a few days longer, that we might visit it again. We enjoyed the quiet of the scene for an hour, talking over our plans for the future, and then started for the harbor. We had gone but a short distance when we discovered Miles Grimsby and Captain McFordingham approaching us.

"They run together now," said Larry.

"I see they do; but I didn't more than suspect it before," I replied.

"I would rather avoid than meet them," added Larry.

"So would I," and turning to the lfet, we took a path which would have led us away from our quarrelsome acquaintances.

But Miles and the captain quickened their pace, and soon placed themselves in front of us, so that escape, without actually taking to our heels, which both of us regarded as rather undignified for the owner and captain of a first-class yacht, was impossible.

"I am glad, gentlemen, that you have accepted the summons contained in my letter of last evening," said Captain McFordingham.

"What letter?" asked Larry.

"My letter."

"I have received no letter from you, or any one else, for that matter, since I came to the Bermudas."

"Then why are you here?" demanded Captain McFordingham.

"We came out for a walk."

"Am I to understand that you deny having received my letter, in which I referred you to my friend, Mr. Miles Grimsby, who is here present, to act for me?"

"I did not receive it, and have no idea of its contents," answered Larry.

"Perhaps it is of little consequence whether you received it or not, since you are here with your friend," added the captain, magnificently. "I trust you are prepared to give me the satisfaction I require."

"I don't quite understand you."

"In one word, my note to you was a challenge."

"In another word, then, I decline it," answered Larry, promptly and decidedly.

"Am I to understand that you refuse to give me the satisfaction that a gentleman has a right to demand?"

"That depends upon the nature of the satisfaction demanded."

"You insulted me —"

"Excuse me, sir; I did not insult you. The statement is absurd."

"Absurd?"

"Ridiculously so."

"You declined to drink with me, and did drink with another."

"I did not drink with another."

"Mr. Grimsby, may I appeal to you?"

"The glasses were all filled, and I noticed afterwards that they were only half full. I presume they drank," replied Miles, sourly.

"It is useless to argue the point, Larry," I interposed. "Let us return to the town."

"Not till you have given me the satisfaction I demand," bullied the tall captain. "Recognizing this gentleman as the one who spoke to you during our interview, he was kind enough to be my friend." And he bowed to Miles.

Captain McFordingham went over the argument by which he reasoned himself into the belief that he had been insulted. Of course we understood now that the fellow had been employed by Miles to provoke a quarrel with Larry, and to make the most of it. The time seemed to be chosen just at the moment when the Unicorn was to sail for New York.

"I decline, on principle, to engage in a duel," said Larry.

"But if you don't give me satisfaction, I shall be compelled to take it," replied the captain, loftily.

"Though I refuse to fight a duel, I know how to defend myself when attacked, replied Larry. "I am not a non-resistant."

"I took you for a brave man; I trust I shall not find you a coward."

"I am not coward enough to fight a duel. If I have done wrong, I can ask God to forgive me; if I have injured my fellow-man, I can ask him to forgive me."

"We are losing time," interposed Miles, nervously, as he glanced at his watch. "If there is any business to be done here, let it be done at once."

"The gentleman who has insulted me is evidently a coward," said the captain, with a sneer.

"I have nothing to do with your quarrel, and am here only as your friend, Captain McFordingham. My time is precious," added Miles, producing a pair of large pistols. "I suppose Captain Farringford is to be regarded as the friend of Mr. Lawrence Grimsby."

"I am his friend."

"Let us walk over to the cliff, where we are not likely to be disturbed," replied Miles, as he led the way.

I followed him, and in a moment we were on the rock overlooking the sea, with a precipice beneath us.

"You have the choice of weapons, Captain Farringford; but, as it was not supposable that you would choose anything but pistols, in these days, I brought nothing else. Will you examine them?"

"I will;" and I took the two pistols in my hand.

"Are they loaded?" I asked.

"They are not. In an affair of honor the pistols should be loaded in the presence of both seconds," replied Miles.

"Have you any other pistols with you, in case I decline to accept these?" I asked.

"I have not. They are regular duelling pistols, and to reject them would be to resort to a mean subterfuge."

"Precisely so," I replied, tossing them over the cliff into the sea.

"Villain!" exclaimed Miles, rushing upon me.

"Mild words, if you please," I replied, holding up my hand to him, to deprecate any violence. "If you lay your hand on me, I'll throw you over after them."

Miles retreated a step, and shouted to his principal. He was apparently afraid that I would put my threat in execution. Captain McFordingham stalked up to the place where I stood, though, as "discretion is the better part of valor," I deemed it advisable to retreat a short distance from the edge of the cliff.

"You called me, Mr. Grimsby," said he.

"I did," replied Miles; "and I have to announce a piece of treachery on the part of Mr. Lawrence Grimsby's second—"

"I object to being called a second. We did not come here to fight a duel, and have no intention of being forced into such an affair." I interposed, for, now that the pistols were at the bottom of the sea, I thought it better to insist upon our views of the subject.

"Captain Farringford has thrown the pistols overboard," continued Miles.

"Thrown them overboard—has he?" And the face of the tall captain lowered. "Cowards!"

"That's a cheap expletive," I answered.

"Honorable dealing was not to be expected from cowards," sneered Captain McFordingham. "Of course we are not to submit to any such trifling as this. Our honor is wounded, and satisfaction is denied us."

Larry laughed; he could not help it. Perhaps he would not have laughed if I had not thrown the pistols overboard. But I sympathized with him, though other considerations had some effect in controlling my risibles. The affair was a farce; but I could not forget that my friend, and not myself, was the subject of wrath.

"Come, Larry, we will return to the town," said I.

"Not yet," interposed Captain McFordingham. "I am not to be trifled with. I have been wounded in my honor, and, as satisfaction is denied me, I intend to take summary vengeance. Mr. Lawrence Grimsby, my affair is with you. Captain Farringford is only your shadow. When he has paid me six pound ten for the pistols he threw into the sea, I shall have no further claim upon him."

"May I ask what you mean by summary vengeance?" asked Larry, with a pleasant smile.

"I mean to flog you, as you deserve. I mean to teach you that a gentleman cannot be insulted with impunity. I mean that your cowardly conduct shall not escape its just retribution."

"I do not purpose to be flogged, Captain McFordingham, in spite of the fact that you are one foot taller than I am. I wish to avoid a quarrel, and I hope to be able to do so. Speaking of cowards, in my opinion you and your second, as you call him, though he is really your principal and your employer, came out here to do me harm. You dogged me, and are determined to force a quarrel upon me. Permit me to say that I regard your conduct as cowardly in the extreme."

"Do you mean to insult me again?" demanded the bully.

"I was only arguing the point. You expressed your opinion on cowardice, and I claim the privilege of expressing mine," replied Larry, with his usual good nature. "Having done so, I shall bid you good morning once more."

"Stop, sir!" said the captain, in a voice which was intended to be very stern and dignified.

Larry walked towards the town, and I started to follow him. The tall ruffian, finding that no further attention was given to him, laid his hand violently upon my friend's coat collar. I sprang forward to assist him, for he was a couple of rods ahead of me.

"Stop," said Miles to me. "You cannot interfere with this quarrel any further;" and at the instant he laid his hand upon me.

I shook him off in the twinkling of an eye, whereat he sprang upon me again, his anger excited to the maddest pitch. I struck him then, but not till then, and he went down, for, trembling for the safety of Larry in the hands of such a giant as the bully, my blow was a heavy one. I rushed towards my friend then, but saw that he had no need of any assistance from me. He stood at bay, pointing at his antagonist the revolver, which I had insisted he should carry in his pocket. I had the mate to it myself, and I produced it now, as Miles, picking himself up, rushed upon me with a stone in his hand. The pistol had a cooling effect upon his ardor, and he halted. I do not know whether the scene, in its present phase, was to be regarded as a serious or a ludicrous one; but Larry and I each covered his man with the muzzle of the revolver. The weapons had a marvellous effect in dampening the ardor of the fierce combatants. We were masters of the situation.

"Then you are prepared to assassinate us," said Captain McFordingham, eying the revolver of my friend.

"I hope you will not make it necessary for us to resort to so unpleasant an expedient," answered Larry. "It is your next move, gentlemen."

"Being armed yourselves, you threw our weapons into the sea," replied the captain. "Doubtless this is your idea of honorable conduct."

"I do not know that it is of any use to waste words," added Larry. "You introduced yourself to me yesterday with the intention of provoking a quarrel. On the most ridiculous pretence you chose to consider yourself insulted. You came out here with pistols; but I don't believe you intended to fight a duel any more than I did. You have not the courage to stand up before a loaded pistol. If you purposed to go through the form of a duel, it was your intention to fire before the word was given, or in some other manner to do the villanous work of your employer. You have my view of the matter, and I have nothing more to say, except to inform you that I am prepared to defend myself under all circumstances."

"You are in a situation to insult me just now. If we ever meet again — and we shall meet again — I shall teach you what it is to insult a gentleman. It is cowardly to point a revolver at an unarmed man."

"It would be if he were not an assassin," replied Larry. "Come, Phil. The business of this occasion seems to be finished, and we may adjourn."

With the pistols still in our hands, we walked slowly towards the town. Neither Miles nor his agent offered to follow us.

"That was a bold act of yours, Phil, but it saved the day for us," said my friend.

"Throwing the pistols overboard was a very simple expedient; and I could think of no other way to stave off the consequences," I answered. "The sooner we get away from this place, the better."

In a short time we reached the landing-place, where we found Lady Eleanor and her friends prepared to embark.

CHAPTER XV.

IN WHICH PHIL AND LARRY WITNESS THE CAPTURE OF A MAN-EATER.

WITH our passengers came the governor and other friends to bid them adieu on board the yacht.

"We have been waiting for you," said his excellency.

"We were detained by a disagreeable incident near Cherrystone Hill," replied Larry.

"A disagreeable incident!" Pray, what was it?" asked the governor.

"It was nothing less than an attempt to compel me to fight a duel."

"Mr. Grimsby, of course."

"He was not to be the principal, for I don't think Miles considers it prudent to stand before the muzzle of a loaded pistol," laughed Larry; "so he employed a gentleman who claims to be your excellency's friend to do the business for him."

"My friend! Who could it be?"

"His name is Captain Gregory McFordingham."

"Pshaw!" exclaimed the governor, contemptuously. "He is a convict, sentenced to transportation for ten years."

"Whew!" added Larry, glancing at me. "But he was a captain in India, I understand."

"Never. Possibly he was a soldier in the Indian army. I don't know. He was the footman of Viscount Bergamot, and was sent here for robbing his master. In the distinguished families where he has been employed he picked up a knowledge of high life, and a vocabulary of high-sounding phrases. Somebody here nicknamed him the captain. He is not without abilities; and, as his sentence had nearly expired, he was permitted to carry on business for himself in buying and selling vegetables. He shall be taken care of."

We assisted our guests into the boats, and on the way to the yacht Larry related our adventure to the governor. It was as evident to him as to us that McFordingham had been employed by Miles Grimsby; and he promised to arrest both of them on his return.

"But Miles will leave in this steamer," suggested Larry.

"I will see that he does not," said the governor.

"I hope your excellency will not detain him," added my friend. "He can do us no harm now; and, as he is my cousin, I have no desire to have him punished."

"You are too lenient towards him. I half expected to hear of a challenge after the affair at my table."

"I don't think Miles himself indulges in challenges," added Larry. "But, please, don't detain him; if you do, the blame of it will rest upon me. I only hope you will not permit the captain to leave the islands, as he intends to do."

"He is well known on board of the steamer, and her officers would not dare to take him."

Our party went on board of the yacht, where we lunched. Lady Eleanor was in high spirits, and was more delighted than ever with her stateroom, which had been put in order for her use. The steamer was still in the harbor, though she seemed to be all ready to sail. The governor's boat came alongside the yacht, and his excellency took leave of his friends. Our fore and main sails were set, and the anchor hove short.

"Heave up the anchor!" I called, when Larry told me he was ready. "Stand by the jib-halyards."

"Anchor aweigh, sir," reported Mr. Spelter.

"Hoist the jib!" I added.

As we caught the gentle breeze, and the yacht began to move, our passengers waved their handkerchiefs, and the governor returned the salute. I saw that his excellency pulled to the steamer; but I was confident that Miles had not yet gone on board of her. The pilot took us safely through the intricacies of the navigation, and we were soon in ten fathoms of water outside the islands.

"Keep her north-east by east," I said, as I gave out the course.

"No'th-east by east, sir," replied the quartermaster, at the wheel.

"This is perfectly delightful, Mr. Grimsby," exclaimed Lady Eleanor, when the pilot had left us.

"I think so myself," replied Larry.

"It is so much pleasanter than a steamer! There is no clanging of machinery, and no odor of oil. Really it seems to me like sailing in a fairy barge."

"We must not crow till we get out of the woods," I ventured to suggest. "If we should have such a storm as we had coming down, I'm afraid your ladyship would not enjoy it."

"I like storms; they are so grand and beautiful," she replied.

"What's that boat?" asked Larry.

It had just come out from behind a reef, and contained two men. I examined the persons in the boat with a glass.

"One of them is McFordingham," I said, when I had made out the long, lank figure of the captain.

"Then Miles must be the other," added Larry. "What are they doing out here?"

"They have come out here to take the steamer, without a doubt. Probably they were afraid the governor would hear about the affair at Cherrystone Hill, and put them in the calaboose for their conduct."

"But the steamer won't take McFordingham, who is a convict."

"Certainly not."

"Pray what's that black thing in the water?" asked Lady Eleanor, as she pointed to an object only a few yards astern of the yacht.

"That's the back-fin of a shark," I replied.

"Isn't that the same fellow that was waiting for

me the other day?" asked Larry. "I should certainly have dropped into the water if Captain Garboard had not shown me that shark."

"Is it really a shark?" added her ladyship.

"There isn't the slightest doubt of it."

"A regular man-eater, too," said Mr. Spelter.

"I should like to see more of him," continued Lady Eleanor, straining her eyes to make out the outline of the fish, which swam on the surface of the water.

"So should I," replied Larry. "I don't want that fellow to follow us all the way to England. He's a blackguard, and a dangerous companion. If any one should be so unfortunate as to fall overboard, the rascal would gobble him up."

"It is a bad sign to have a shark following a vessel," said Spelter.

"I don't care for the sign, but I don't like the fellow," added Larry.

"But I can't see him," said Lady Eleanor.

"We will catch him if you say so, Mr. Grimsby," continued the mate.

"Can you do it?"

"To be sure we can. Our owner last year used to go a sharking every season down to Nantucket and the Vineyard. We have all the gear on board — shark-hooks, grains, lances."

"Catch him, then. Sharks are the natural enemies of mankind — the pirates of the ocean," replied Larry.

"Mr. Cheeseman, you can get up the shark-hooks, and rig the tackle for that fellow," said the mate.

"Ay, ay, sir," answered the second mate, apparently pleased with the anticipated sport.

"That's a big fellow," continued Mr. Spelter. "He isn't less than twenty feet long, and may be thirty. He would bite a man in two as a chicken does a worm, and only make two mouthfuls of him. He is an ugly fellow."

"That he is," I replied. "A bigger one than that followed the Michigan, when I was in her, for a week. Shall we lower the mainsail, Mr. Spelter, and haul him in over the stern?"

"Yes, sir; but we must kill him before we get him on deck, or he will break things. I have no doubt he weighs twelve or fifteen hundred pounds."

"Probably he does. Lower the mainsail and top up the boom. We can rig a snatch-block under it, and then swing him in by a rope made fast to his tail."

The mainsail was lowered and carefully secured. The boom was topped up as far as it would go, and the snatch-block rigged under it. The shark-hook was a very large one, with a fathom of chain attached to it, so that the voracious monster should not bite off the line. It was then made fast to a strong rope, and baited with a strip of salt pork. Cheeseman, as he was an old hand at the business, took the line, while six of the crew were mustered on the quarter-deck to assist. Mr. Spelter stood by with the grains in his hand, to be used when the shark was hauled up. Larry had given his arm to Lady Éleanor, and they stood at the taffrail, where they could witness the whole operation to the best advantage.

"There comes the steamer," said Larry. "That boat is hailing her."

"I see she is," I replied.

Even the interest we all felt in the capture of the shark did not prevent me from watching the boat. The steamer stopped her wheels, and one of the two men was taken on board of her. Through the glass I saw McFordingham attempt to go up the accommodation ladder, but he was driven back into his boat. The steamer started her wheels again, backing, apparently to avoid some rock towards which she was drifting. I could not help uttering a sharp cry when I saw the wheel strike the boat, for I expected to see the tall captain crushed beneath it. But the wheels stopped, and McFordingham pulled out of the way. I could just hear the sharp words that followed, and then the steamer started on her voyage. The boat, instead of pulling towards the harbor, headed for the yacht. The sea was smooth, and there was hardly a breath of air. I saw that what I should call a thunder-shower at home was coming up in the west, and, as it might be attended by a squall, I was rather anxious to have the shark disposed of; though, as the wind was dying out, we could hardly increase our distance from the islands before it came.

Cheeseman dropped the baited hook in the water, and the shark had swum up to it as soon as it touched the surface. He toyed with it for a moment, and then, rolling over upon one side, he took it into his mouth. After waiting a moment until the monster had the bait fairly between his

teeth, the second mate gave a tremendous twitch, and fairly hooked the game. The line had been passed over the snatch-block on the boom, and the six men on the quarter-deck had fast hold of it. The instant the shark felt the hook, he commenced a series of the most violent struggles, lashing the water to a white foam. His struggles were fearful, and Lady Eleanor was glad to retreat from her position at the taffrail.

"Now, walk away," said Cheeseman, when the shark was hooked.

But it was not so easy, even for six men, to walk away with the line. The entire crew had come aft to witness the sport, and half a dozen more of the hands took hold of the rope. The shark was slowly raised from the water; but not for an instant were his fierce struggles intermitted. He came up with his mouth wide open, exhibiting his rows of frightful teeth, which it made us shudder to look upon. He was not yet in position to be lanced, and Spelter went forward for something. I saw him go below, and presently he returned to the quarter-deck with a shovelful of live coals from the cook's stove.

"What's that for?" demanded Larry, sharply.

"I am going to give him a dose of hot drops," replied the excited mate, laughing at the idea which he was in the act of carrying out.

"What do you mean?"

"I'm going to throw this shovelful of live coals down the shark's throat," answered the mate, pushing his way towards the taffrail.

"Stop, Mr. Spelter," shouted Larry, sternly.

"Yes, sir. I'll wait for you, so that you and the lady can see the fun," added the mate.

"I don't want to see it. Stop!"

"What, sir?"

"Don't you do it. Throw the coals over the side. I will have nothing of that kind done here."

"Why not, sir?"

"The shark shall be killed, but not tortured. I won't have anything like cruelty perpetrated before my eyes."

Mr. Spelter threw the coals over the side, and seemed to be amazed and sheepish at the interference of the owner.

"Kill the shark as quick as you can, Mr. Spelter," added Larry. "Don't torture nor torment him."

"I never saw anybody before that was willing

to take the part of a shark," replied the mate, as he took the long lance in his hand.

"I do not believe in cruelty to any animal; and I will not suffer it in my presence, when I have the means to prevent it," said Larry.

By this time the shark had been hauled up snug to the snatch-block. But he still struggled fearfully.

"Now punch him, Mr. Spelter," said Cheeseman.

"That I will," replied the mate, as he thrust the lance into the shark, and repeated the operation a dozen times.

After a while — and it was a long while, for the monster held on to life with wonderful tenacity — the shark was killed. Lady Eleanor had an opportunity to examine him at her leisure, and we decided not to take him on board. One of the men cut away the hook from his mouth with an axe, and the carcass of the shark dropped into the water, to be the food of others of his kind.

During the excitement over the shark I had kept a sharp lookout upon the weather. I had sent a couple of hands to lower the jib and flying-jib, and to stand by the foresail-halyards. There was not a breath of air, and I was satisfied that we should have a smart squall.

"Blanche, ahoy!" shouted a voice from astern of the yacht.

I turned, and saw McFordingham pulling with all his might towards us. The bow of his boat was badly stove.

"Haul down the foresail," I shouted, as I discovered the squall coming down upon us.

At this moment McFordingham came alongside, and leaped upon the deck of the yacht. Of course I could not object, for his battered boat could not have stood it for five minutes in a sharp sea. The lightning flashed and the thunder roared as I had seldom seen before. Along the sea something like a great cloud of fog seemed to sweep on its way towards us. In an instant it overtook us. It was the squall, stirring up the water and driving the spray in the air as it advanced.

"Hard down your helm!" I called to the quartermaster, as the blast struck the yacht.

She came up head to it, and we looked into the teeth of the squall. As every sail was furled, it did us no harm, and was over in a few moments. Then the rain poured down in torrents, and our guests fled to the cabin; but Lady Eleanor declared that the squall was magnificent.

CHAPTER XVI.

IN WHICH PHIL AND OTHERS ARE CONFOUNDED BY A MYSTERY.

I DID not go below when the rain began to pour down in torrents, but clothed myself in a rubber suit, and kept a sharp lookout for any peril that might be lurking near the yacht. I had too often walked the deck in storm and gale to heed the exposure. Drifting astern of us I saw the battered boat of McFordingham, now half full of water; but its late occupant had gone below. If he had not been on board, I should have hoisted sail, and laid our course again; but I could not think of carrying the fellow off from the penal servitude to which he had been sentenced, even if I had been willing to endure his presence during the voyage. It was my intention to run up to the entrance of the harbor, and put him on shore.

In half an hour the rain ceased to fall, but we

heard the thunder still booming down to leeward of us. I called all hands, and set the jib and mainsail, under which, with a gentle breeze, we ran towards the islands again. McFordingham, without any invitation, had gone below as soon as he came on board. It was not necessary for me to ask him to explain his movements since we parted at Cherrystone Hill. He had not deemed it prudent to return to the town after the events on the cliff. Perhaps, if I had not taken the precaution to throw the pistols overboard, Larry, and possibly myself, might have been shot; and, with no particular warning from the governor, Miles and his companion might have departed in the steamer before our absence was discovered by our friends. As my friend and myself went to the town first, it was not safe for them to do so; and they had taken a boat at some other point, intercepting the steamer as she came out. Miles had been received on board, but a passage was refused to his companion, though, as I saw myself, he had persisted in attempting to go up the side of the vessel, apparently after the order to back her had been given. I concluded that he had pulled for the Blanche with the expectation of going to England in her.

"Where is that man?" I asked, when we had got under way.

"Who — Longshanks?" added Spelter.

"Yes. We must get rid of him."

"In the forecastle, I suppose, sir."

"Send for him."

In a few moments the convict appeared. As he came up the ladder I saw him look about him, and he did not seem to be pleased when he discovered that the yacht was headed towards the islands.

"At your service, captain," said he, touching the little cap on his head. "You sent for me."

"I did."

"But allow me to suggest that your yacht is headed the wrong way," added he.

"Our course, just now, is laid for your benefit. I believe no invitation was extended to you to come on board of the yacht."

"You are quite right, Captain Farringford; and for this breach of courtesy I must tender my apology," he replied, bowing with respectful deference.

"Why did you pull for the Blanche when you were nearer the shore?"

"Because I saw that squall coming, and couldn't pull against it. I should have been swamped in a moment, with the bows of the boat stove in. Your extensive knowledge of maritime matters will enable you at once to see the force of this argument."

"You had time enough to pull to the shore before the squall came."

"I could not know how much time I had. Besides, I desire to visit England; and that steamer barbarously refused me a passage, which I trust your good-nature will not permit you to do."

"You over-estimate my good-nature, Captain McFordingham. Your excellent friend, the governor, informed us that you were a convict, serving out a penal sentence in these islands, for robbing your master, Lord Bergamot, whose footman you were."

"I acknowledge that I was the victim of a conspiracy. I was not the footman of Lord Bergamot, — you see to what slanders the unfortunate are subjected, — but his confidential steward. His lordship was a young man, and wild, very wild, Captain Farringford. He got into a broil in London, one day, with another nobleman, and the case went to the courts. Unfortunately, I was called as a witness, being with my lord at the time of the quarrel. His lordship was the aggressor, and all the blame properly rested upon him. Under the sanctity of an oath, what could I do but tell the truth? I appeal to you, Captain Farringford, to say whether I could avoid speaking the truth. As a gentleman, I always speak the truth. But especially should a gentleman do so under the sanctity of an oath. Do you see any way, captain, that I could avoid speaking the truth? I did speak the truth, the whole truth, and nothing but the truth, which, as a gentleman, I always do. Lord Bergamot was convicted of an aggravated assault, and, besides a heavy fine, was sentenced to prison for thirty days, just to convince the common people that viscounts are no better than other citizens before the law in England. Mark the consequences, Captain Farringford. During the absence in prison of my lord, I took care that his property should suffer no waste; and, having sent a portion of his plate and jewelry to a place of greater security, I was prosecuted for embezzlement, and sentenced to ten years' transportation. I give you the simple fact, captain, and leave you to judge whether I am a criminal or not. I incurred the wrath of Viscount Bergamot, and here I am."

"Of course you have told that story to your excellent friend, the governor," I added.

"I have, sir; but he is an official under the government, and must do his duty. I honor him for it, sir. But his excellency is fully convinced of my innocence, and has honored me with his confidence and sympathy. Though it would not be becoming in him, as the representative of Her Majesty in these islands, to say so, yet the greatest favor you could do him would be to extend to me an invitation to visit England in your magnificent yacht."

"I'm sorry I cannot oblige his excellency in this particular. You seem to have forgotten the events in the vicinity of Cherrystone Hill," I suggested, amused at the brazen effrontery of the fellow.

"Under the circumstances I am willing to accept the apology of your friend, and to acknowledge entire satisfaction for what has passed," he replied.

"Are you, indeed? You are very obliging."

"I assure you, I bear no malice. When I give my hand, my heart goes with it."

"Doubtless you are very affectionate."

"I am naturally of a confiding nature; and I am willing to own that this has led me into mistakes and indiscretions. But I cherish no malice. I accept the apology of your friend, and I should give him and you my entire confidence, unreserved, and without a thought of ill."

"You are very kind. I suppose it does not occur to you that it was at all irregular to waylay us at Cherrystone Hill, with the intention of shooting us," I suggested.

"Everything was to be fair and upon honor. Perhaps my wrongs have made me sensitive. Your refusal to drink with me was an insult; your declining to deal with me aggravated my wrath, and your refusal to give me a passage, with the ridicule of your friend of my manly proportions, stung me to the soul. I know I am sensitive; my wrongs have made me so."

"But you were the agent of Mr. Miles Grimsby."

"I beg your pardon; I was not. We lodged at the same house. He told me his wrongs; that your friend had robbed him of his title and estates. With my confiding nature I could not withhold my sympathies from him. Fired with indignation, I sent you a challenge. We met."

"We met by accident on our part; and I think your excellent friend, the governor, will put you in the calaboose when he sees you."

"Perhaps his sense of duty will compel him to do so; but it will be against his better judgment and his sympathies. I hope you will not subject him to this unpleasant necessity."

"I certainly shall."

"You will wrong him and me."

"I feel obliged to take the responsibility."

"One word more, captain. Perhaps my sympathies were too gushingly extended to Mr. Miles. I am inclined to think, now, that they were. But Mr. Miles communicated to me, in the strictest confidence, while we were waiting in the boat for the steamer, his plans for the future. He means harm."

"And you are willing to help Mr. Lawrence out?"

"I will defeat the plans of Mr. Miles, though I cannot betray his confidence. A gentleman has a sacred regard for the confidence reposed in him. Your friend will lose his life in the most mysterious manner, when Mr. Miles is a thousand miles away from him," added the convict, dropping his voice down to a whisper. "I can save him."

"Well, I hope you will do so, if you have an opportunity."

"All I ask is a passage to England, and —"

"I will send you ashore in a boat as soon as we are off the mouth of the harbor."

I turned on my heel and walked aft to Larry, who was talking with Lady Eleanor and her friends. I told him what the convict had said. Of course it was all fiction, and we laughed at it. The sun had come out again, and all hands were on deck. I ordered a boat to be got ready to convey the convict to the shore. Half an hour later we came up into the wind off the "Boiler," and the boat was lowered into the water.

"Now, give my compliments to Captain McFordingham, and inform him that the boat is at his service," I said to the mate.

"Hadn't you better appoint a committee to wait upon him, Phil?" laughed Larry.

"Perhaps that would be the more elegant way to do the business; but I have sent the mate."

"Suppose he don't accept your polite invitation, Phil," added Larry.

"Then I will appoint the committee, consisting of the three stoutest fellows in the vessel, to coax him," I replied.

"Don't use violence, Philip."

"Shall I permit him to remain on board the Blanche in case he declines to accept my invitation to go on shore?" I asked.

"You always pose me with hard questions, though I have repeatedly declared that I am no philosopher. But use your own judgment, Philip."

"I don't put my judgment against positive orders. But the fellow does not seem to show himself; and I suppose he refuses to go on shore."

Mr. Spelter had gone below, and had been absent fifteen minutes. I concluded that he was arguing the question with McFordingham. I was willing that he should exhaust his logic, and I waited patiently for the issue. In another quarter of an hour the mate came on the quarter-deck.

"Well, Mr. Spelter, where is he?" I asked.

"Mr. Longshanks has gone up, sure," replied the mate, with a puzzled expression on his bronzed face.

"Gone up? What does he say?"

"I haven't heard him say anything," replied Spelter, scratching his head.

"Didn't you give my compliments to him?"

"I did not. The fact on't is, I can't find him."

"Can't find him?"

"No, sir; can't find him. I've looked in every hole and corner, and so have the cook and stewards. I should say he had crawled into some pipe-stem, if we had one on board long enough."

"That's very singular," I added.

"Singular! 'pon my word it's marvellous."

"The fellow didn't jump overboard — did he?"

"Not that I'm aware of."

"You broke his heart by your coldness, Phil, and he has gone over into the drink in despair," laughed Larry. "Have you overhauled the foreto'-bobbin, Mr. Spelter?"

"No, sir, not yet."

"Have you opened the fore royal hatch-way?"

"No, sir. We never open that except in presence of the owner," answered the mate.

"Right! Always be prudent, and don't incur any needless responsibility."

"What's the fore royal hatchway, Mr. Grimsby?" asked Lady Eleanor.

"Really, I don't know. You must ask Captain Farringford."

"It's where the foreto'-bobbin comes into juxtaposition with the main-to'-gallant bobstay," I replied.

"That's it. Phil knows all about marine matters," added Larry. "But, Mr. Spelter, where is our elegant friend, Captain McFordingham?"

"I don't know, sir, unless he has gone overboard, and a shark has gobbled him up."

"He went below, and of course he is there now," I added. "Send half a dozen hands down to look for him."

I went into the cabin myself, and, with the steward, made a thorough search of that part of the vessel. I looked into the lockers, under the berths, and even invaded Lady Eleanor's stateroom. I then went through the other apartments, and joined the hands in the forecastle. I examined every place where it was possible for a man to be concealed, but could not find him.

"Who saw him last?" I inquired.

No one answered, but the hands looked from one to another.

"I saw him go down the ladder to the forecastle, after talking with you, sir," replied Butters, at last, when I had repeated the question.

"Who was in the forecastle then?"

"No one, I think, sir. All hands were on deck."

"Did he go on deck again after that?"

"I didn't see him, sir."

"Did you see him, cook?"

"No, sir. My door was closed, and he didn't come into the kitchen," replied the cook.

As the fugitive could get from the forecastle to the cabin only by passing through the kitchen, I concluded that he must be in the forward part of the vessel.

"He may have crawled into the hold," suggested Mr. Spelter.

"Open the hold," I replied. "Steward, a lantern!"

The Blanche was a keel vessel, and not a centre-board, and there was some space below the floors, where the ballast and the coarser provisions were placed. Two of the men had been appointed to take charge of the hold, whose duty required them to see that it was kept clean, and that the boxes, barrels, and bags were secure.

"The tall man was down there before," said the head steward.

"The man we are looking for?" I asked.

"Yes, sir. I bought some fruits and vegetables of him; and he offered to go into the hold and stow them so that they would keep well."

The two holdmen went down into the dark recess below. I followed them myself, to see that they did their duty faithfully. I saw them turn boxes and bags, and I looked in every part of the hold myself. Then we went through the search a second time. I looked for myself into every part where a man could be concealed, without success. I did not overhaul the ballast, which was of pigs of iron, packed each side of the keelson, secured against shifting by timbers bolted to the ribs, for no man could live with such a weight upon him. Reluctantly I gave up the search.

We were all confounded by the mystery. We lay off and on till the next morning without being able to solve the strange problem, and then laid our course for the voyage. Again and again we searched every part of the yacht. I even went around her in a boat, to see if the fellow was not concealed under the counter, or clinging to the bobstay. I finally concluded that he had dropped overboard, and swum ashore, to avoid being handed over to the governor.

CHAPTER XVII.

IN WHICH PHIL AND LARRY ARE ASTONISHED, AND THEN ARE ASTONISHED AGAIN.

ON the morning after the strange disappearance of McFordingham, the wind was fresh from the westward, which gave us our best point in sailing. The Blanche seemed to fly on her course, and we soon took our last look at the Bermudas. Our passengers were not seasick, and Lady Eleanor had no abatement of the pleasure of the voyage. Larry was very funny, and made his guests laugh a great deal. Our German instructor, Mr. Schmidt,— who has thus far been ignored because there was nothing for him to do or say,— was called into action, and we had German conversations in the forenoon and afternoon, in which Lady Eleanor joined. We were very serious in this business, and our teacher was faithful. In the evening we had reading and games in the cabin.

For a day or two the mystery of the convict was occasionally alluded to, and Larry expressed his belief that the captain had evaporated into mist, and had been wafted off to sea. He thought that, if we ran into a fog, the captain would again assume shape and substance, and drop down upon our deck.

"You mean by that, you think he will appear again," I replied.

"I'm afraid he will, Phil. I advise you to keep clear of all fog-banks," laughed Larry. "In nautical parlance, give them a wide berth."

"It is utterly impossible that he should be concealed on board," I protested.

"Of course. I don't expect to see him until a fog-bank settles down on the Blanche; then you will see him just as the fisherman did the genius, forming from the smoke that issued from the urn. That's the way he'll come back. Therefore, keep clear of fog-banks."

"I don't know that it is possible to keep clear of them, Larry."

"Then we may be doomed to endure the captain's presence during a portion of the voyage," laughed Larry.

But the subject was dropped in a couple of days, and we ceased to think of the captain. We studied German, played checkers, chess, and backgammon, and read Tennyson, Scott, and Longfellow. The days passed away very pleasantly, and time hung no burden on our shoulders. For five days we had the wind from the westward, and made steamer time of it; but then came a calm and a fog. For a day and a night we kept the fog-horn sounding at intervals. It was cold and disagreeable on deck, and for this reason I was separated most of the time from our passengers. Yet we had but twenty-four hours of this weather, and on the sixth day out, the fog rolled away in the middle of the afternoon, and the sun shone brightly upon the ocean, drying up our decks, and bringing warmth to the heart as well as to the air. The wind came from the north-west, and again the Blanche leaped on her course, with every rag of canvas drawing. Our party were seated on the quarter-deck enjoying the scene.

"Well, Larry, we got out of that fog safely," said I, as I took a camp-stool opposite my friend, and facing the helmsman. "The captain hasn't turned up yet."

"Don't crow till you are out of the woods, Phil," laughed Larry, as he pointed to the dense fog-bank in the south-east. "The tall man is certainly in that pile; you may depend upon it."

"Perhaps he is; but I think we are clear of that bank. If the captain is in it, he will find it rather difficult to work his way up to windward so as to reach our present position."

"Not at all, Captain Farringford," said a voice behind me.

I sprang to my feet.

"I told you so, Phil. I knew the fog would bring him," exclaimed Larry, laughing heartily.

I turned and saw Captain Gregory McFordingham standing on the weather side of the mainmast. He had just raised his little cap, and was in the act of making his politest bow to the party.

"I am exceedingly happy to find that my coming was not unexpected, and I hope it will not be unwelcome," said the captain, bowing and smirking again.

"May I be so bold as to ask where you came from?" I added.

Raising his long arm, he shrugged his shoulders, and pointed to the fog-bank, with the most melodramatic effect.

"I knew it, Phil," exclaimed Larry. "He has been in that fog-bank all the time."

"You are quite right, Mr. Grimsby; and a very disagreeable situation it was, too, I assure you. I humbly hope and trust that the inhospitality of your friends will never compel you to take refuge in a fog-bank," added McFordingham, shaking his head ruefully.

"How long have you been on board, my excellent friend?" asked Larry.

"I have been on board some time, sir; in fact, an hour or two. You see, I had some difficulty in shaking off the fog and getting clear of it. But I got hold of your mainmast and held on with all my might. After a fearful struggle, which has left me quite exhausted, I disengaged myself, and came down the mainmast."

"You seem to be rather the worse for the wear," I added.

"Well, I am. This life in a fog-bank is very uncomfortable. I hope you will never be obliged to endure a week of it, as I have, Captain Farringford. I have lived on air and cold water all the time; and I hope you will order your steward to give me something more substantial."

" You shall be fed," I replied.

" And a little drop of brandy would not come amiss."

" We don't use the article; but you shall have tea or coffee."

All hands had gathered in the waist, and were regarding the tall captain with the utmost astonishment. I called the second steward, and told him to feed our unexpected guest. He took him to the kitchen.

" Where did that fellow come from?" I asked of the wondering crew.

" About five minutes before he showed himself to you, he rushed up the fore-hatch, and then placed himself by the mainmast, where you couldn't see him," replied Butters.

" But where was he concealed?"

" I don't know, sir."

No one knew. I called the hold-men, and went below. I examined the hold again, to find the place where the captain had stowed himself. Everything appeared just as it had been at my former visits. The boxes, bags, and barrels were all in order, and did not appear to have been disturbed. I looked at the ballast, which was piled up in the run, over the top of the keelson. Every pig of iron seemed to be in the same position as when I had last examined it. I returned to the deck, more amazed and bewildered than ever. I made further inquiries among the men; but they were all on deck when McFordingham appeared. One of the hold-men had brought up a sack of potatoes that afternoon.

"It's very singular, Larry," said I, when I had related to the party on the quarter-deck the result of my examination.

"Not at all, Phil," laughed Larry. "He came out of that fog-bank, as he told you. The poor fellow has been enveloped in that mass of cold moisture for a week. Didn't he tell you what a struggle he had with the mainmast to shake off the fog?"

"I'm sorry he didn't stay in the fog," I replied. "If I had known he was wrestling with the main-topmast, I would have cut it away rather than have him come on board again."

"You could not have been so cruel, Phil."

"I don't understand it," I continued, vexed by the mystery.

"It is perfectly plain, my dear Philip. You are

a philosopher, I know; but you should not fill your head with vain inquiries. Accept the only plausible explanation of the mystery, and fill away again on the other tack, with the foreto'-bobbin taut on the weather skysail bobstay."

"The fellow must have been on board all the time."

"Quite impossible. The fog condensed him on the main-topmast, and he slid down like a drop of water. Now we have him, let us make the best of him," said Larry.

By this time the captain had finished his meal, and appeared upon deck again.

"Captain McFordingham, we have gone too far on our cruise to return with you; and, as you are going to England with us, you may inform me where you were concealed," I began, as he coolly seated himself near our party.

"As Mr. Grimsby has already explained the matter very fully, it would not be proper in me to invalidate any of his statements," replied the captain, bowing and touching his cap to our owner.

I saw that the rascal did not mean to tell me what I desired to know, and Larry pretended to be perfectly satisfied with the solution already given. My dignity would not permit me to press the question, and I let it drop. The captain never for an instant abandoned his magnificent speech and manner, and the party were very much amused by him.

The next day the lookout forward announced a sail ahead. Such an event always makes a sensation on board; and for an hour we speculated over the nation and character of the approaching vessel, before she was near enough to be made out. She proved to be a large steam frigate, under sail only, belonging to the British navy.

"She is bound to the West Indies," said the mate.

"Then she will go to the Bermudas, without doubt, for there is a naval station there," I added. "Set the colors."

The American flag went up to our peak, and we saw the red cross of England on the man-of-war.

"If she is going to the Bermudas, we can give Captain McFordingham an opportunity to return in her," I suggested to Larry.

"As you think best, Phil," replied he.

The frigate was close-hauled, and not making

more than two knots an hour, for the wind was light. I gave the order to come about and stand over towards her.

"Where is McFordingham?" I asked.

"He was asleep in the forecastle just now," replied Butters.

I went into the forecastle to announce my intention myself. I found the captain in the temporary bunk which had been fitted up for him. I waked him with a pull at his collar.

"I beg your pardon, Captain Farringford," said he, springing to his feet. "What can I do for you, sir?"

"There is an English man-of-war in sight, bound to the south-west. I have no doubt she is going to the naval station at the Bermudas. As this will afford you an excellent opportunity to return to your friends, I suggest that you take passage in her."

"Thank you, Captain Farringford. You are very kind to take so much trouble on my account," he answered, apparently unmoved by my announcement.

"Not at all; don't mention it, my dear captain. We are running down to the ship, and shall speak her in a short time."

"As you are aware, I desire to visit England; and I couldn't think of giving you so much trouble on my account."

"I beg to assure you it will be no trouble at all. We shall be particularly happy to serve you in this manner."

"Very well, Captain Farringford; you are so very kind that I cannot deny myself the privilege of accepting what you so graciously offer. I will be at your service in a few moments, if you will permit me to take a lunch before I bid a last farewell to so many kind friends."

"Certainly, captain;" and I passed through the kitchen to give the cook an order to supply him with food.

The cook was not at his galley; and I went on deck by way of the cabin. All hands were looking at the man-of-war, and the cook was among them. He had come on deck to ask one of the hold-men to bring him up a supply of vegetables for dinner. He and the hold-man went below. In ten minutes the cook came to me on deck again.

"Where is the captain, sir? His lunch is ready," said he.

"I left him in the forecastle."

"He is not there now, sir."

"Not there?"

"No, sir."

I looked about the deck, and he was not there. I descended by the fore scuttle to the forecastle. Certainly the rascal was not there. I began to snuff another mysterious disappearance, and I was vexed, sorely vexed. The news that McFordingham was not to be found had been passed along till it reached Larry, who came down the fore scuttle, shaking his sides with laughter at what he was pleased to call a repetition of the old joke.

"We have no fog to-day, Phil," said he. "He couldn't have gone off in a fog this time."

"I think not," I replied, biting my lips with vexation.

"But, Phil, don't hail that English man-of-war till you find the man," added Larry; "they will think you are making fools of them, and won't appreciate the joke."

"I shall not hail her till we find the captain," I replied.

At this moment the hold-man opened the scuttle leading into the hold, which was in the passage by the door of the ice-house. He came up with a lantern in one hand and a basket of vegetables in the other.

"Frinks, is the captain down there?"

"I didn't see him, sir," replied the man.

"How long have you been in the hold?" I asked.

"Five or ten minutes, sir; just long enough to get out these beets and turnips."

The cook took the vegetables, and I went into the hold once more, this time attended by Larry. Frinks carried the lantern, and, stooping low, — for the hold was not deep enough to permit us to stand up straight, — we carefully examined every nook and corner, with no better success than before. The ballast had not been moved, but at one end of the pile of pigs of iron was a quantity of cabbages, and some heads of lettuce set in wet sand. I pulled over the heads, but there was no head of a man to be seen.

"He isn't here, Phil," said Larry, whose curiosity seemed to be excited.

"Where is he, then?"

"I haven't the least idea."

We went on deck again. I ordered the English

flag to be hoisted at the fore, and the men to give three cheers in honor of the frigate. The ladies waved their handkerchiefs, to which a group of officers in the rigging replied. We sheered off and laid our course again, the Englishmen, probably, supposing that we had varied it in order to gratify our curiosity.

I was never more perplexed in my life than I was at the sudden disappearance a second time of Captain McFordingham. I was morally sure he was on board, and almost as sure that he was not in the hold. Larry laughed about it, and insisted that the captain was some mighty necromancer, who had the power to make himself invisible when occasion required.

CHAPTER XVIII.

IN WHICH PHIL AND OTHERS SOLVE THE MYSTERY.

THE frigate went on her way, and we soon lost sight of her. She was a beautiful object to look upon in the immense cloud of canvas which she carried, and for an hour, while we were near her, she was a decided sensation. I was sorry I had not been permitted to transfer our unwelcome passenger to her, for I should have felt better if I had known that the tall captain was on his way to his home in the Bermudas. I had directed all hands to keep a sharp lookout below for the missing man. The day wore away, and nothing was seen of him.

At sunset our party were all seated on the quarter-deck, and Lady Eleanor had just favored us with a song, which we rapturously applauded, though, as it was in the higher flights of music, I was unable to appreciate it. But singing was a novelty on board, unless I except the rude songs of the sailors. The sound of her ladyship's voice attracted the attention of the hands forward, and in a moment the whole crew had gathered near the mainmast to listen to the music. Even the cook and stewards came on deck, and no lady ever had a more attentive audience. As I said, our party on the quarter-deck applauded, and our demonstration was followed by another on the part of the crew, more emphatic than ours. While I was trying to make up my mind whether it was quite proper for the seamen to applaud a performance to which they had not been invited, I discovered Captain McFordingham in the rear of the group, vigorously clapping his hands, and looking as delighted as though the entertainment had been given for his especial gratification.

"Capital!" shouted he. "*Encore.*"

The hands turned and regarded him with a degree of astonishment which appeared fully to equal my own.

"Longshanks!" exclaimed Mr. Spelter, walking up to the fellow.

"Sir, allow me to suggest, in the mildest manner possible, that the epithet you apply to me is exceedingly opprobrious," said McFordingham, with his loftiest air. " Such expressions wound the feelings of a gentleman. Allow me to remind you that my name is Captain Gregory McFordingham, formerly in the service of the Honorable East India Company."

" Exactly so; and I dare say the Honorable East India Company were very glad to get rid of you," replied the blunt mate. " Where did you come from, Gregory?"

" Excuse me, Mr. Spelter, if I decline to hold any further communication with you," answered the captain, with a magnificent sneer.

" Good!" laughed Larry, who had walked forward to the mainmast with me.

" I cannot hold any intercourse with one who has not the instincts of a gentleman."

" That's rather rich for a convict," said Spelter, who did not enjoy the airs of the fellow as our owner did. " I don't think I could cut it quite so fat as that if I had been convicted of robbing my employer."

" As you are beneath my contempt, I can take no notice of your vulgar insinuations," added McFordingham, turning his back to the mate.

"If I had my way, I'd take you down a peg, Longshanks," muttered the mate.

"Where did you come from this time, captain?" I asked.

"I owe you an apology, Captain Farringford, for not coming on deck this forenoon, as I told you I would," replied the fellow, touching his little cap, and bowing low to me. "Permit me to explain my conduct."

"It is hardly necessary."

"But, sir, I owe it to my honor as a gentleman — a gentleman who has been unfortunate, but whose honor was never sullied by the breath of reproach."

"The breath of reproach! That isn't bad, Phil," laughed Larry.

"I repeat it, sir; who has been unfortunate, but whose honor is unsullied. You were so kind, Captain Farringford, as to offer me a passage, in that noble man-of-war, to the Bermudas. I am obliged to you for the invitation, and for the very courteous manner in which it was extended. I intended to accept it; but, upon more mature deliberation, I decided not to do so. It would have been courteous on my part to inform you of my change of purpose; but I trust that, under the circumstances, you will accept my humble apology."

"Where were you when we looked for you?" I asked.

"I was in a safe place," he answered, smiling.

"A direct answer, if you please."

"I must beg your indulgence, Captain Farringford."

He bowed low again, and I saw that he did not mean to reveal his hiding-place. I was vexed, but my dignity would not permit me to press the question. He went below soon after, and I heard of him in the cook-room, cajoling the cook to set before him the best the yacht afforded.

"Sail ho!" called the lookout at a later hour in the evening.

Ahead of us I saw the red and white lights of a vessel, indicating that she was on the starboard tack. As we could not see her green light, there was no danger of a collision, and we held our course, showing her our red light on the port side, and the white light at the foremast-head, for the Blanche was provided with these signals, though at that time but few sailing vessels carried them.

"I shouldn't wonder if that was another man-of-war bound to the West Indies," said Mr. Spelter, though I could not see what reason he had for suggesting the idea.

"Possibly," I replied, indifferently.

"I feel rather confident she is a man-of-war," added the mate. "If she is, she must be bound for the Bermudas; and I hope you will give Longshanks another invitation to go home."

"I certainly shall."

Spelter walked forward and aft, and in a few moments it was reported through the yacht that the sail approaching was a man-of-war, bound to the south-west. The mate was so confident in his opinion in regard to the vessel, that I went to the forecastle and informed the captain that he must be ready to take passage in her. He was polite, as usual. Most of the watch below went on deck to see the vessel, and no one was left in the forecastle, so far as I could see. Of course I expected another mysterious disappearance, and I did not mean to be cheated this time. I went to the fore scuttle and ascended the steps, but I paused and seated myself on the combing of the hatch, where I could see McFordingham. In another moment he rose from the bunk where he was seated, and moved aft. I hastened down again; but the fellow had already vanished. I looked about, but could see nothing of him. He must have entered the midship passage, from which the doors of the cook-room, ice-house, and mate's room opened. I walked in this direction, and was immediately confronted by Cheeseman, the second mate.

"He has gone into the hold, sir," said he.

"Did you see him?" I inquired.

"Yes, sir. I am here to watch him," answered the second mate, as he took down the lantern which was suspended from a deck-beam in the forecastle.

We had searched the hold so many times that I could hardly believe the captain's hiding-place was there. At this moment Frinks, the hold-man, came down with a lantern and a basket in his hand.

"Where are you going?" I asked.

"Into the hold after some potatoes for breakfast," replied the man, as he opened the scuttle in the midship passage.

I made a gesture to Cheeseman to stand back,

and Frinks was permitted to jump into the hold and to close the scuttle after him, as he always did, so that a person coming out of the cook-room or going to it might not fall through the opening.

"Now open it, Cheeseman," I said to the second mate.

He did so, and I jumped down into the hold. Cheesman followed me with the lantern. Bending low, as I was obliged to do, I went aft, where I found Frinks at work on the heap of cabbages, which he seemed to be placing on the end of the pile of ballast. McFordingham could not be seen.

"Frinks, go on deck and tell Mr. Spelter I wish to see him in the hold," said I to the hold-man.

"Ay, ay, sir," replied Frinks; but he did not go.

"Do you hear me, Frinks?"

"Ay, ay, sir; but—"

"Obey my order at once," I added, sternly.

The man went; but I was satisfied that he knew more than he chose to tell, and had connived at the concealment of the convict.

"Throw those cabbages off the ballast, Cheeseman," I continued, and assisted him in the work.

In a few moments Mr. Spelter appeared, accompanied by Frinks.

"I don't think that's a man-of-war, now," said the mate, chuckling, as he joined us. "But who has been overhauling this ballast?"

"I was not aware that it had been overhauled."

"Yes, it has. I had this ballast stowed under my own eye; but I don't know that I have been in the hold before since we sailed from New York."

Spelter assisted in throwing off the cabbages; but when they had all been removed, the convict was not to be seen.

"He wasn't under them," said Cheeseman.

"Who, sir? the tall gentleman?" inquired Frinks. "He's not down here, sir."

"Who moved the ballast, Frinks?" demanded the mate, savagely.

"I moved it a little, sir, just to make a place for the sand-box, so that it shouldn't shift in a sea, sir — that's all," replied the hold-man.

"Lift up the box and slide it aft," I added, confident that we had found the burrow of the fugitive.

"There's nothing under it but the ballast, sir," said Frinks.

"Lift it up."

It was a shallow box, partly filled with sand, in

which the lettuce was set up. The two mates lifted it and moved it aft.

"That's what's the matter!" exclaimed the mate, triumphantly. "This is the fox's hole."

When the box was removed it revealed a square opening in the pile of ballast, and in the aperture we discovered the head and shoulders of Captain Gregory McFordingham, who immediately drew his long body out of the hole under the ballast, and sat up before us.

"Did I understand one of you gentlemen to say that the vessel approaching is not a man-of-war, bound to the south-west?" said he, with admirable self-possession.

"Possibly she is, possibly not," I replied.

"I am not partial to British men-of-war on long voyages. I have had some experience in them," added the captain. "I find they are not comfortable or pleasant for those who have the instincts of gentlemen, especially if they have been unfortunate. I have been unfortunate, and my proper position in society is not generally recognized."

"Well, now, I thought it was," added Mr. Spelter. "Were you not sentenced by the court to ten years penal servitude in the Bermudas?"

"Permit me to say, Mr. Mate, that I decline any further intercourse with you."

"Well, I don't decline any further intercourse with you. If you don't come out of that hole in the twinkling of an eye, I'll snake you out, like a bug from a rug. Come, stir yourself, Longshanks," said the mate.

"Captain Farringford, I appeal to you against this fellow's assumption," added the captain.

"Obey his orders; he is the mate."

"But I am not one of the crew."

"I don't regard you as a passenger. Come out, and you will save trouble."

"Tumble up here, Longshanks," added Mr. Spelter, as he made a demonstration towards the captain.

McFordingham concluded not to wait for any further action on the part of the mate, but crawled out of his hole. Then we had an opportunity to see how his den had been constructed. The pigs of iron, which were from two to three feet in length, had been removed from the middle of the pile, till there was an aperture seven feet long, and deep enough to contain the gaunt carcass of the fugitive. The sides on the interior had been carefully built up. Across the top of the recess thus formed the pigs of ballast had been laid, except at one end for about two feet, which had been covered by the sand-box. The bottom of this den had been covered with straw, which had been used for packing various articles in barrels and cases.

"That makes a soft thing of it," said the mate. "But it's lucky for you, Longshanks, that we haven't had any rough weather, or some of that ballast would have been rolled on your stomach. In a gale of wind we might have had those pigs tumbling about the hold."

"The place was very comfortable for a few days," added the captain; "but I don't like it for steady lodgings."

"Of course Longshanks didn't do this job alone," added the mate to me.

"I beg to inform you that I did," interposed the fugitive with dignity.

"Frinks helped him, and knew he was here," I replied.

"No doubt of that," added Cheeseman.

"No, sir; I didn't know he was here," answered the hold-man.

"A lie won't help you," I continued. "We will go on deck."

The mate called several hands, and stowed the ballast in a safe manner. In the forecastle I called the cook.

"Did you send down after potatoes?" I inquired.

"No, sir," replied the cook, petulantly. "That man has brought up more potatoes than I can use in a week. I made him carry back a lot of them this forenoon."

"Frinks, how much did the tall man pay you for what you have done for him?"

"He gave me five sovereigns, and promised me five more if he got safely to England," growled the hold-man. "But he told me that you and Mr. Grimsby wanted him to go in the yacht, but you were afraid of offending the governor, and would be much obliged to me if I helped him off."

"You were a simpleton to believe him. Give him back his money," I replied.

Frinks gave him the five sovereigns, which McFordingham did not object to receive. They had made the arrangement when the purveyor brought the vegetables on board, and McFordingham was to have been concealed before the vessel sailed; but the affair at Cherrystone Hill had rendered it dangerous for him to show himself in the town. He was refused a passage in the steamer, and then fell back upon this arrangement.

The scheme which had led to the discovery of the convict's hiding-place had been invented by the mate The approaching sail was not a man-of-war; and the second mate had been stationed in his room to watch the movements of McFordingham after he had been told that he was to be transferred to her.

"I have had quite enough of you, McFordingham," I said to the convict, when I had settled the matter. "Mr. Spelter, if this man goes abaft the foremast, either on deck or below, put him in irons."

"I will," replied the mate.

I was not aware that there were any irons on board; but I was afraid the fellow had a mission with Larry, which he might attempt to execute.

CHAPTER XIX.

IN WHICH PHIL AND LARRY SET OUT ON A LONG TRAMP.

I BEGGED Larry not to take any further notice of McFordingham, for even the mock consideration extended to him inflated his vanity and induced him to take liberties which were intolerable to me, and especially so to the mate, who disliked "Longshanks" with an intensity which bordered on hatred. Mr. Spelter kept a sharp eye upon him, and, I think, would have been very glad to catch the fellow abaft the foremast, for the sake of giving him a little wholesome discipline; but Mac was prudent, and did not furnish the opportunity.

Our voyage was pleasant and prosperous, without an incident worthy of note after the events described. The routine of life on board was about the same every day. We ate, drank, slept, read, played our games, and were quite as happy as we should have been on shore, without the wonders of the sea to instruct and improve us. Lady Eleanor appeared to enjoy the trip to the end, though I think she began to weary of it before we arrived at our destination. Larry was very attentive to her, and I am afraid, if Blanche Fennimore had been on board, she would have been just a little jealous, because ladies can't help such feelings; though, if she had been present, there would probably have been no occasion for jealousy. We had some rainy weather, and a mild gale; but there was nothing that could be called severe. For half a day we were under jib and reefed mainsail, but the reef was only to save the nerves of the ladies.

In twenty-one days from the Bermudas we were at anchor in King's Road, near the mouth of the Avon, for the wind and tide did not permit us to ascend the river to Bristol. We landed our passengers and their luggage at Portishead.

"If you please, Captain Farringford, I will land here, and not trouble you to carry me up to Bristol," said McFordingham, as the boats were ready to depart from the yacht.

"I think you had better content yourself for a while longer on board," I replied. — "Shove off."

The boats pushed off. I had bidden adieu to our passengers, but Larry went ashore, intending to accompany them to Bristol.

"As I am an unwelcome guest here, I am anxious to relieve you of my presence," added McFordingham. "It is not agreeable to the feelings of a gentleman to be in the company of those who do not want him."

"You should have considered that question before you came on board," I answered.

"Circumstances alter cases."

"They do; and they alter this case so that you can't go on shore till your friends come to receive you."

"I don't understand you, Captain Farringford."

"As the matter now stands, you are an escaped convict. I do not intend to incur the charge of having assisted you to escape."

"My time has expired."

"I don't know whether it has or not. Let others decide that question. I shall hand you over to the authorities."

"Captain Farringford, I have had the highest

opinion of you as a gentleman and a man of honor; and I did not think you capable of this degree of cruelty," added the captain, his jaw falling at the announcement I made.

"Do you think I would throw such a villain as you have proved yourself to be upon the community?"

"Sir! I permit no man to call me a villain," exclaimed the convict, straightening up his long body.

"It is quite time that we speak the truth. You went out to Cherrystone Hill with Miles Grimsby, armed with pistols, to waylay and murder our owner or myself, or both of us. There is no other name than villain in my vocabulary for a man who does such a thing."

"Sir, I went out, as a gentleman, upon an affair of honor."

"That's enough. We will not argue the point."

"You called me a villain, Captain Farringford, and I demand satisfaction," cried the captain, shaking his fist in my face.

"I'll give you satisfaction," said Mr. Spelter, who, with the second mate, laid violent hands on him, and tied his arms behind his back. "You are abaft the foremast."

"This is an outrage upon a British subject," sputtered the prisoner.

"All right, my hearty," replied the mate, as he made him fast to the rail on the forecastle.

The boats returned, and the next morning we ran up the Avon, and went into the dock at Bristol. When the pilot went ashore, he sent a couple of officers on board, and McFordingham was handed over to them. He said but little now, when he found that fine speeches were unavailing.

"Captain Farringford, you might have made a friend of me; but you have chosen to be my enemy. I am your foe now; and, when you and your friend least expect it, I shall be with you," said he, as the officers were coming off. "My time is out, and I shall not be sent back to the Bermudas. I shall only be vexed and annoyed by your conduct."

I do not know but this fellow thought himself an injured man; he talked and acted like one. The officers took him; but, unhappily, we had not yet seen the last of him.

"Frinks," I called, as soon as the captain had been removed.

"Here, sir," replied the hold-man.

"We don't want you any longer," I continued.

"I shipped for the voyage, sir."

"I will not have a man on board who is not faithful to his employers. You have been guilty of conspiracy in making our owner and the officers liable for assisting a convict to escape; and you have endangered the safety of the vessel by moving the ballast. I am ready to go to the American consul's with you, and execute the necessary bond."

"I didn't mean any harm," pleaded the man.

I went on shore with him, and the consul decided that I had good cause to discharge him. He gave me his written and sealed consent to the discharge. I paid Frinks more than he was entitled to receive; and I hope he left with the feeling that it is always better to do right than wrong.

Leaving the yacht in charge of Mr. Spelter, I went to the hotel with my valise, where I was to meet Larry. Our passengers had already departed, and we were soon on our way to Bloomridge, the seat of the Grimsbys. I need not say that Larry was cordially and affectionately greeted by Sir Philip. The baronet was intensely indignant at the conduct of Miles; and I am sorry to say that he used some bad language in his anger.

"I'll disinherit him! I'll cut him off with a shilling," protested Sir. Philip.

"Don't do it, sir. Give him a fair half of all you have to divide between him and me," pleaded Larry.

"I will not. He is a bad boy. Let him earn his bread by the sweat of his brow. The rascal has been borrowing large sums on the credit of his future prospects. He shall be a beggar yet," stormed the old gentleman.

"He has done his worst now," added Larry. "I beg you will not punish him for anything he has done to me."

"He is a bad boy. He don't deserve anything of me, and certainly he don't of you. It is a pity he didn't go to the bottom in his yacht."

Larry had been turning the leaves of a large clasp Bible that lay on the centre-table, as Sir Philip paced the room. He raised the book and read,—

"'Ye have heard that it hath been said, Thou

shalt love thy neighbor, and hate thine enemy. But I say unto you, Love your enemies, bless them that curse you, do good to them that hate you, and pray for them which despitefully use you and persecute you; that ye may be the children of your Father which is in heaven; for he maketh his sun to rise on the evil and on the good, and sendeth rain on the just and on the unjust.'"

The baronet paused opposite Larry as he began to read. His lip quivered, and I thought he would fly into a passion with his grandson. He listened a moment. Larry was reverent and gentle in his manner and his tones. Before he had finished reading the passage, I saw that Sir Philip's anger had passed away. Larry closed the book, and the baronet dropped into his chair without another word.

"If Miles had fired a bullet into my head, and I had only one brief moment to live, I should thank God that I had not tried to injure my cousin; that in my heart I had forgiven him," said my friend.

"I dare say you are right, my boy; indeed, I know you are. We will think of the matter again," replied Sir Philip.

We staid at Grimsby Hall a week, and then returned to the yacht at Bristol. However interesting the details of our cruise from this port, around the south of England, to the coast of Norway, might be, I have not the space to give them. We put into various harbors; we spent a week in the Isle of Wight; we wandered on the beaches at Margate; we poked our noses into Boulogne-sur-Mer; we left the yacht at Flushing, and, after a run through Holland, joined her again at the Helder; and then made a long stretch to Bergen, where we arrived late in June. At Cowes we saw the Hermia, and learned that she was for sale, because Mr. Fitzgerald was tired of yachting. She had arrived about the time the Blanche did, which made her passage a week longer than ours.

We were delighted with the Norwegian coast, and especially with the Fjord, through which we made our way to Bergen. We found two English yachts at anchor there, but we did not visit them, for we were in haste to commence one of the tramps upon which we had so long exercised our imaginations. We had purchased everything which pedestrians could need, and packed the articles in knapsacks. Gayly we strapped them on our backs, and set out upon our long tramp. The Blanche, in charge of Mr. Spelter, was to sail round the coast to Frederiksværn, and await our arrival. We had spent a day in Bergen, and started early in the morning.

We had our "sea legs" on, so that walking was not an easy thing at first. The earth was unsteady under our feet, and kept rolling and jerking. After a tramp of five miles we agreed that we were tired. Seeing a brook a short distance from the road, we seated ourselves upon a rock on its bank, where we could refresh ourselves with a drink of water. We ate a slight lunch of sausage and English biscuit.

"We are a handsome couple, Phil," laughed Larry. "We have been talking about this tramp through Norway for months, and now we are tired out after a walk of five miles."

"I expected to be very tired at first," I replied. "I never could walk a great distance after coming from sea; it makes my legs ache. But I notice that after a half hour's rest I am as good as new."

"But have you any idea that we can make thirty miles a day?"

"Certainly I have; forty if we choose, after we

are broken in. I met a gentleman last year at Dresden who told me he had walked fifty miles in a day. When we get our sea legs off we shall be all right."

"I hope so, for I enjoy walking when I am not too tired."

"We have only about a dozen miles to walk to-day, and then we take a boat."

"I am ready for the boat now," laughed Larry, as he lay back on the rock and closed his eyes.

At this moment I heard the rattle of a couple of carioles, which soon passed in the road near us. They were occupied by Englishmen, and were going at a furious pace, and I could not see the faces of the travellers; but I noticed that one of them was a remarkably tall man, and that the other wore a Scotch cap.

"Larry, who are those people?" I asked, as my companion started up.

"How should I know?" he replied; "I haven't been introduced to them."

"But look at the tall fellow."

"I see him."

"He has a big red mustache and bushy red hair."

"I'm willing."

"Well, I think you have been introduced to him."

"Possibly. Who is he?"

"In my opinion it is Captain Gregory McFordingham, who promised to appear to me when I least expected to see him."

"Of course the other fellow is Miles, then."

"Very likely."

"But I don't believe it. It is too absurd. How could Miles and that tall flunky be here?"

"I don't suppose they are here by accident; if they were it might be strange. Do you flatter yourself that Miles is done with you?"

"I did think we were rid of him."

"Not yet. The rascal will follow you, or send some one after you, till you are out of the way. Norway is just the place for his operations."

"How could he be here?"

"Easily enough. I have no doubt he reached England before we did, even if he had to wait a week in New York for a steamer. Perhaps he came here in one of those yachts we saw at Bergen. I am sorry we didn't ascertain more about them."

"But how should he know where we were going?" asked Larry, who seemed to be rather troubled by the situation.

"We stated our plans very clearly at the table of the governor in the Bermudas. You said we should take a tramp from Bergen to Christiania, by the way of the Vöringfos and the Rjukanfos. Then we talked it over with the yacht people at Cowes. I fancy that Miles knows just where we are going."

"Grant that Miles might be here; the captain must be on his way to the Bermudas before this time," added Larry.

"Doubtless the fellow sent for Miles when he was in limbo. If the rascal's time was out, perhaps he was discharged. The Hermia was for sale when we were at Cowes, and very likely Miles bought her for this excursion. Don't you think we had better change our route, Larry?"

"Not I, my boy. I won't dodge Miles and his flunky. But perhaps it is fortunate that we brought our revolvers," replied my friend, decidedly.

After resting an hour, we resumed our walk, as fresh as in the morning. Before noon we reached a post station on one of the fjords whose arms extend far inland, where, after dinner, we took a boat with two rowers. We saw nothing of the carioles or their occupants, who, if they were the persons I supposed, did not appear to be watching us very closely.

CHAPTER XX.

IN WHICH PHIL AND LARRY VISIT THE VÖRINGFOS, IN NORWAY.

WE seated ourselves in the boat, in which we were to spend the afternoon, and had shoved off, when a cariole dashed up to the station-house on the shore.

"Boat ahoy!" shouted a familiar voice.

"That's Spelter!" I exclaimed, making signs to the rowers to return, for I could not speak a word of their language. "I wonder what has happened."

"Perhaps the Blanche has sunk or burned up," suggested Larry.

"Of course something has occurred, or he wouldn't run after us."

The oarsmen pulled back to the shore, where we found the honest mate in a state of high excitement. We supposed he had sailed from

Bergen before this time, and was on his way to Frederiksværn.

"What's the trouble, Mr. Spelter?" I demanded, as we landed.

"Trouble enough, sir," replied the mate, looking as solemn as an owl. "I couldn't sail without letting you know the news."

"Well, what is the news?" asked Larry, laughing. "Has the foreto'-bobbin broke down, or the main-royal backstay given out?"

"I don't think it's any laughing matter, Mr. Grimsby, though you may."

"You don't give me the means of judging yet," added Larry. "If you will tell us what the trouble is, we shall know whether to laugh or cry."

"Well, sir, Mr. Miles Grimsby is on your track again," said the mate, delivering himself as though he had dropped a bombshell at the feet of his employer.

"No; we are on his track, for he has gone ahead," replied Larry. "Of course you are aware that McFordingham is his interesting companion."

"Yes, sir. I came out here to tell you these

facts; but you seem to know them, and I'm sorry I came," muttered the mate, disappointed because he had failed to produce a decided sensation.

"My dear Mr. Spelter, you have done just the right thing at just the right time, and I am grateful to you for your interest and sympathy. We happened to obtain a glance of Miles and his tall satellite as they drove by in carioles. We were sitting on a rock, out of the road, and I am confident they did not see us. We thought it even possible that we were mistaken. You have settled the matter finally and conclusively. You have done your duty faithfully, as you always do, and I commend you."

"I was afraid they might drop down upon you with a blunderbuss or a pair of pistols, as they did in the Bermudas," answered the mate, satisfied with the commendation of Larry.

"Exactly so. But tell us what you know about them," said Larry.

"While I was waiting for the tide to turn, so that we could go to sea, I thought I would pass the time of day with the two yachts that lay in port. The first one I went to was the Hermia; and the first man I saw on board of her was

Frinks, the man we discharged. He was impudent and saucy, and I wanted to wring his nose for him. He told me you didn't make much by discharging him; but I said we got rid of him, and that was all we wanted. He wished to make it out that he was better off than in the Blanche, and was glad to get out of her. Then he couldn't help telling me that Longshanks didn't go back to the Bermudas, for a pettifogger had got him out of the scrape for five pounds, and that Longshanks had given him back the money you made him return. They went to Cowes together, where they found Miles, who had just bought the Hermia. While I was listening to the fellow, Osborne came out of the cabin, and I found he was the sailing-master of the yacht."

"Miles has a pleasant company," said Larry.

"Well, sir, I knew what they were here for, and I went ashore as fast as four oars could pull me there. I knew you had started on your tramp, and I found that Miles and Longshanks had gone the same way. I didn't like the looks of things. The landlord of the hotel where you were told me all about it, and I made tracks after you. Don't you think I'd better go with you on this tramp?" asked Spelter.

"What for?"

"Well, I should like to get hold of Longshanks once more. I would make him wish he was in the Bermudas again."

"I dare say you would, my marine friend; but discretion is sometimes better than zeal. I think I can take care of myself; but I am grateful to you for your kind intentions. Now you may return, and sail as soon as you are ready. You need not inform your friends where you are going," replied Larry.

"Not I. I listen, and keep still, myself. I suppose the Hermia will follow us wherever we go; but, if she isn't faster than I think she is, she will have to sail by faith rather than by sight."

"Right! I'll trust you anywhere, Spelter. Good by," said Larry, as we returned to our boat.

The mate watched us till we were out of sight. Of his fidelity there could be no doubt; and the honest fellow evidently did not like to have us incur the risks before us without his aid. At nine o'clock in the evening, though the sun was still above the horizon, we arrived at a place called Evanger, where we spent the night. We found a couple of Englishmen here, one of whom told us that two travellers, one of them very tall, had left for Vossevangen two or three hours before.

"Of course they were Miles and the captain; but I don't understand their game," said Larry.

"They know we are going to the Vöringfos, and perhaps intend to wait there for us."

"They may have to wait a long time," laughed Larry.

In the morning we started on foot for Vossevangen, about twelve miles distant. The scenery was delightful, and we spent the whole day on the road. When we reached our destination we found capital quarters at the post station, which was on the bank of a small lake. The landlord spoke English very well, and had no guests in his house. Miles and the tall man had staid there the night before, and hastened on early in the morning.

"They inquired for two young men," added the landlord.

"Have you seen the young men?" I asked.

"Yes; they went forward the day before, and were going to Ulvik."

Larry laughed, and thought "two young men" was rather an indefinite description.

We liked the hotel and the landlord so well that we remained at this place three days, one of which was Sunday, when we had the opportunity of seeing the people of the village at church in their best clothes. We went trouting one day in the lake, and the next in the river which flows into it. We were realizing all we had anticipated, and we almost forgot Miles and his tall flunky. Again we set out on our tramp. We were now accustomed to the solid earth, and walked twenty miles in one day, which brought us to Ulvik. The "tall man" had not been there, and it was probable that Miles had gone from Eider directly by boat to Vik, which is the place from which excursions are made to the Vöringfos. We went to Vik; the enemy had been there before us, and were at the falls; had gone the day before, and were expected to return that night. We engaged a guide and a boat for the next day. We learned that there was a kind of shanty at the falls, where four persons could sleep very comfortably; and we decided to pass one night there, for the walk up and back was too tiresome to be made in one day.

We crossed the lake the next morning, and commenced our up-hill tramp. By noon we reached the falls. The scenery was the wildest we had ever seen. There were precipices two thousand feet high, and chasms twelve hundred feet deep. The Vöringfos itself is a cataract, which falls in one sheet about nine hundred feet. It was sublime; and we were deeply impressed by the wild grandeur that surrounded us, which towered above, and was spread out beneath us. We stood on a shelf of rock which extended out over a chasm more than a thousand feet deep. Peder, our guide, had a piece of whale-line, about twenty-five feet long, the ends of which we secured around our bodies, while the bight of it was passed around a small pine tree. Thus guarded against any accident, we lay down on the rock and gazed into the abyss beneath us, while Peder went to the shanty to procure some milk for our lunch.

"That's a big hole, Phil," said Larry, as we lay on the rock, surveying the depths below. "If a fellow should tumble over, it would be apt to wrench him a little."

"Don't try it, Larry," I replied; "it would make your head ache."

"I think it would. But this is really the grandest thing I ever saw in my life."

"Well, I don't know about that. It is high and deep, but it is not equal to Niagara."

"There's not so much of it, I know; but it's a big thing."

"No doubt of that."

I heard footsteps on the rock near me; but, supposing the guide had returned with the milk, I did not look behind me, being fascinated by the wild scene before me. Suddenly I felt a sharp pull on the rope. I supposed it was one of Larry's practical jokes.

"Don't fool in such a place as this," I protested.

The pine tree around which the rope was passed sent its branches out so far that I could not see my friend without rising.

"I'm not fooling," he replied.

"Didn't you pull the rope?"

Before I could receive an answer, the rope was jerked again with so much violence that I was pulled back from my place. I sprang to my feet, the strain of the rope still bearing upon me. At the same instant Larry made a violent movement. I grasped the tree for support. As I turned, to my horror I encountered McFordingham, and found that my friend was over the precipice, and supported only by the rope. The tall villain had a pocket-knife in his hand, and I saw that he intended to cut the line. Larry was struggling at the rope, to draw himself up, and, if I had not held on at the pine tree, he would have dragged me after him.

When I rose from my reclining position over the chasm, I let out nearly half the length of the line, and my friend dropped that distance below the edge of the cliff. With my left arm around the pine, I took from my pocket the revolver I carried.

"If you touch that rope you are a dead man," I shouted to the convict.

"I only desire to save your friend," replied McFordingham.

"Begone!"

I pointed the pistol at him, and he retreated. Suddenly the pressure on the rope ceased, and my heart came into my mouth. I pulled at the line, but there was no longer any weight upon it. I drew it up, and found that the knot in the end, by which the loop had been secured, was untied.

I threw myself upon the ground in utter horror and despair. My poor friend had dropped into the abyss beneath. The cold chills swept through my frame, and the blood seemed to be frozen in my veins. Why had I not compelled Larry to shun this place while that tall fiend was on his track? Why had I permitted him to come here, when I knew that Miles and the captain had not returned to Vik?

McFordingham stood at a short distance from me, where he had halted when I lowered the pistol. He looked terrified rather than guilty.

"May I speak to you, Captain Farringford?" said he.

"You have done your work," I cried.

"I have done nothing. I went there to warn you of the peril of that place," replied he, in loud tones. "Poor Miles perished there yesterday, and —"

"Miles!" I exclaimed.

"Will you hear me?"

"I will." And I walked towards him.

"You will not believe that I could do so awful a deed as you say I have. Upon my honor as a gentleman —"

"Did you say that Miles fell over the precipice?"

"Yesterday. Our guide is below now, looking for his remains. That is a very dangerous place; and when I saw you and your friend,—I did not know who you were,—I seized him by the legs. He kicked me, and in his struggle slid off the edge of the precipice, just as Miles did. They are together now," replied McFordingham, wiping his eyes with a very dirty handkerchief.

I could not believe the villain's story, but because he told it rather than because it was improbable in itself.

"What were you doing with the knife in your hand?" I demanded.

"I was going to cut the rope," he replied, boldly.

"Cut the rope?"

"Yes; cut the rope, for I expected to see you go over after him, and I was determined to save one of you, if I could not both."

"Why didn't you take hold of the rope and help me haul him up?"

"I was afraid he would drag me over after him. If you had seen your best friend go over into that awful abyss, you would have felt as I did."

"I do not believe a word you have said," I added.

"You wrong me, Captain Farringford."

"You told me you would appear at a moment when I least expected to see you; and you have."

"I will not argue the matter. I attempted to save your friend, and I should have done so if you had not threatened me with your pistol just as I was going to pull him up."

"Villain! you were going to cut the rope, just now."

"If I could not save him, I should have cut it, in order to save you. You wrong me. I desired only to serve you both. If I had known who you were, I would not have gone near you," muttered the wretch. "I knew that the rock on the edge of the precipice keeps breaking off, and letting people fall over; but you did not. I saw my poor friend go over, and I would save even my worst enemy from such a horrible fate."

I went back to the cliff, and lay down on the spot which Larry had occupied. I trembled and groaned with horror as I thought of him, lying mangled and dead in the abyss beneath. Was it even possible that Miles had met with a similar fate? I could not yet believe it. I was bewildered, almost crazy, as I tried to discover the body of Larry in the dark depths beneath.

"Phil!"

It was the voice of my friend, and apparently not ten feet below me. My heart leaped again.

"Where are you, Larry?" I called.

"Here," he replied, "all right."

"O, Larry!" I exclaimed.

I turned, and found that the captain had departed.

CHAPTER XXI.

IN WHICH PHIL RESCUES LARRY FROM A VERY PERILOUS POSITION.

THE events which had occurred on the brink of the precipice were all compressed into the space of less than a minute — far less time than it requires to relate them. From the instant that I felt the first jerk of the rope till it ceased to bear upon my body, was hardly an instant. The branches of the Norwegian pine between Larry and myself prevented me from seeing him, and from seeing the captain when he appeared. At the first jerk of the rope I had spoken to my friend, and he had answered me, so that he could have had no suspicion of anything wrong until he went over the precipice, and was dangling above the deep abyss, held up only by the rope. Of course, when the pressure ceased, I concluded that he had fallen into the depths below.

Horror and despair filled my soul then, though the intelligence imparted by McFordingham, that Miles had been the victim of a similar calamity, for an instant diverted my thoughts. I could see no reason why the villain should make such a statement if it were not true. Perhaps it was made to startle me, and throw me off my guard, in order to prevent me from using the pistol in my hand. I was confident that the exhibition of this weapon had saved me from being thrown over the precipice, though I was unable fully to comprehend the plan of the villain.

I heard the voice of Larry. It was his voice, though it was rather hoarse and unnatural. The sound of my own name made my heart leap. My friend assured me he was all right, and I thanked God that he was still safe, though I knew not in what peril he might be at that instant.

"Where are you?" I asked, a second time, as I looked over the cliff, and endeavored to see him.

"Here; I'm safe," he replied, in a kind of gasping tone, which alarmed me, in spite of the assurance his words contained.

"I don't see you," I replied.

"Do you see the bush below you?"

I saw a little stunted pine, whose top projected beyond the rock which overhung the chasm. Grasping the doubled rope, which still passed around the pine on the cliff, I leaned over as far as I dared. About ten feet down I discovered a shelf in the rocks, hardly more than a foot wide, on which stood Larry. From a fissure behind it grew the pine, to which he was clinging for life. My heart beat wildly when I saw the danger of his situation.

"Hold fast, Larry," I called to him.

"I am all right," he answered. "But I can't hold out here more than a week or two."

It was a ghastly attempt to be funny, and the tones of his voice belied the humor he attempted to cultivate. I drew back with the utmost care before attempting to stand up; but as I did so a large piece of the rock beneath me crumbled off and dropped into the abyss. My blood ceased to flow again, as I thought of the mischief it might have done.

"Larry!" I called, in an agony of doubt.

"All right, Phil," he replied; and I realized that the rock had not struck him. "Don't throw any more of them down, for one may hit me."

I regained my feet. I looked and listened for any indications of the presence of the tall villain; but I concluded that he was satisfied with the work he had done, and had departed finally from the place. I made one end of the rope fast to the pine tree, near its roots, and then tested its strength with the strongest pull I could give. Tying a small stone to the other end of the line, I dropped it over the precipice. I swayed it back and forth till it swung in where Larry could reach it.

"Make it fast under your arms, Larry," I called to him. "Be careful about the knot; your life depends upon it."

He made no reply; but the motion of the rope assured me that he was doing what I required. As he was no sailor, it was a long time before he appeared to be satisfied with the knot he tied.

"All ready," said he at last.

"Are you sure you have made it perfectly secure?" I asked.

"I'll risk it," he answered, in a tone which had suddenly become cheerful — a result which I attributed to his confidence in the rope.

"Are you comfortable now?"

"Not particularly. I should feel better in the cabin of the Blanche," he replied.

"Can you hold on a little while longer?"

"Yes; half an hour."

"I'm afraid I can't pull you up alone. But the guide will be here soon."

"I can haul myself up," he added.

"Don't try it."

"Just as you say, Phil."

My patience was nearly exhausted before Peder arrived with the milk.

"Come, quick!" I shouted, when I saw him at a distance, with a gesture which started him out of his propriety, and caused him to spill half the milk in the vessel he carried.

"What's the matter?" he asked, looking wildly around him, as he placed the little wooden pail of milk on the rock.

"Man the rope, here!" I replied, picking up the line. "All ready, Larry!"

"I'm all right," answered he.

Peder uttered a succession of exclamations in his own language, and flew around like a parched pea in a hot skillet. His stock of English was not very large; and the more I talked to him, the more confused he became. I carefully examined the edge of the overhanging rock, to assure myself that no more of it could be broken off. I overhauled the line to see that there were no weak places in it, and instructed Peder how to do his share of the work.

"Now, Larry, grasp the rope with your hands, and swing off," I called to my imperilled friend.

I heard the straining of the line as he did so, and I could not help trembling when I thought how trivial a mishap might launch him into eternity. Peder and I seized the rope, and raised the precious burden slowly and cautiously, for we were in danger of dashing his brains out on the rock which projected out over the abyss. Swaying the rope out as far as we could, when Larry's head came up to the edge of the cliff, we landed him safely on the top of the rock.

"Thank God, you are safe!" I cried, as I sank down, exhausted as much by my emotions as by the exertion I had made.

Larry breathed heavily, and his face was deadly pale. He crawled a short distance from the precipice, and lay gasping on the rock. Neither of us spoke for some time; and I am sure that both

of us thanked God for his preservation from the depths of the heart. I was the first to recover my breath. The lifting of his weight, at arm's length, over the cliff, had required the outlay of all the strength I had, and for the time I was entirely used up. Peder had been of but little service, for I could not make him understand what he was to do.

"Take a drink of milk, Larry," said I, offering him the pail.

"I'm about played out," he replied, faintly. "That scrape has taken a year's growth out of me."

"I have been scared out of more than a year's growth," I added.

He drank a portion of the milk, and I followed his example. Slowly he revived from his exhaustion. Raising himself from the rock, he sat up. He glanced at the cliff and shuddered. I removed the rope which was fastened to his body.

"I don't want to try that again, Phil," said he, languidly.

"A man fell over there yesterday," added Peder, with a violent gesture, pointing to the rock.

"Who was he?" I asked.

"I don't know. He was with a very long man."

"Miles!" said Larry, with a start.

"How do you know?" I demanded, sharply, for the intelligence seemed to confirm the statement of the captain.

"The people at the house say so," answered Peder. "The rocks break off and let him down."

"How do the people at the house know? Did any of them see him fall?" I inquired.

"No; but the tall man say so."

"That's one good reason why it is not true," I added. "Do you know when the tall man told them so?"

I had to repeat the question in several different forms before Peder understood me.

"Just now — this morning. The long man tell me to tell you he fall over," protested Peder, warmly. "He tell me to tell you the people say so."

"Did the people tell you so?"

"I say, he tell me to tell you the people tell me so; and I tell you so."

"Where is the tall man now?"

"Gone away."

"Gone where?"

"Back to Vik. I tell you what he tell me to tell you," continued Peder, with the utmost simplicity. "He give me two species to tell you what I tell you."

"Did he?" I added, amused at the stupidity of the guide.

"You don't believe it. I show you the money;" and he produced two bills, each of the denomination of a specie dollar.

Larry could not help laughing with me at the simplicity of Peder, who had entirely failed to understand what the tall man required of him.

"Did he tell you a man fell over to-day?" I asked, thinking it possible the guide had made more than one mistake.

"No; no to-day. Yesterday he fell over; the man with the tall man fell over; not this man," replied Peder, pointing to Larry.

I understood it very well. Peder had met Mc-Fordingham, on his return with the milk, and the villain had tried to have his story of Miles's calamity confirmed, perhaps to save his principal from being implicated in the catastrophe to my friend. The captain had not told the guide that Larry had fallen into the abyss; and I was satisfied that the villain had departed from the vicinity in the full belief that he had effectually removed the only obstacle to Miles's succession to the title and estates of Sir Philip Grimsby. I was satisfied that Miles and his bravo would hasten away from the Vöringfos with all possible speed. I was not mistaken, for we neither saw nor heard of them in Norway again.

"You seem to know all about it, Phil," said Larry, after I had compelled Peder to tell all he knew concerning the tall man.

"I do know all about it."

"Do you happen to know how I slipped over that rock?" he asked.

"I do. Don't you?"

"I haven't the slightest idea."

"Do you mean so?"

"Certainly I mean so. I joke sometimes; but I never felt less like doing so in my life than I do at this moment. I felt a twitch at the rope, which I supposed was given by you. Then you told me not to fool in such a place. I replied that I was not fooling, and was on the point of backing out, when I felt another pull at the rope; a piece of the rock broke away under my breast, and the next instant I was dangling over that big hole."

"Did you hear any footsteps on the rock?" I asked.

"I don't know that I did; I don't remember. But somehow I was conscious that there was a person behind me. I supposed it was Peder, and didn't mind him. The rope fetched me up with a sharp turn. Then it was let out, and I dropped down some distance."

"That was when I got up, and stepped back to this tree."

"Reaching out with my leg, I hooked on to a bush, and hauled myself in. I found there was a shelf on the rock, and, with the help of the bush, I got upon it. It was not a good place to stand, Phil," said Larry, as a tremor shot through his frame.

"But how came the rope untied?" I asked.

"I untied it," he answered, with a languid smile.

"What for?"

"Because I knew you were made fast to the other end of it."

"That is the very reason why you ought not to have untied it," I protested warmly.

"I am no philosopher, Phil, and can't argue the question. By the amount of line let out I knew you were near the pine tree; and it occurred to me that if I made a slip I should bring you down with me. There was no need of two of us going down into that black hole; and, as my chance was the poorer of the two, I thought I would cast off the line, and give you an opportunity to patronize some first-class life insurance company, at a proper time in the future."

"Unselfish to the last, Larry!" I exclaimed, grasping his hand, and wringing it warmly.

"Steady, Phil. Clap a stopper on the fore-to'-bobbin. You'll break off my fluke. I'm not one of those fellows who, when they go down in the world, want to drag others after them. My position was not a very comfortable one, and was very trying to the nerves. I felt better after one end of that rope was tied to my body and the other to the pine tree. I have told you all I know about it; now, tell me what you know."

"The pull at the rope, which you and I both felt, was evidently given by McFordingham," I replied. "I have no doubt he has been watching and waiting here for us. I suppose he took hold of the rope, lifted you up, and rolled you over the brink of the precipice."

"I don't see how he could do that, and I not know it."

"He is a very powerful man. He lifted you by the rope, and for aught I know, dropped you over. I didn't see him till your fall jerked me away from the cliff. I got up and grasped the tree. I saw the villain, with his knife in his hand, and I showed him my pistol. He had a wholesome regard for it, and retreated."

"I heard your voice, but I supposed you were talking to Peder," interposed Larry.

"Then the pressure was removed from the rope, and I believed you had fallen into the chasm. I don't want to feel again as I did then. You gave me a shock by casting off the rope."

"Well, my boy, the shock was not so great as it would have been if you had struck the bottom of that hole. If you ever bet, you may bet high on that. I must say, Phil, that I have lost all respect for Captain Gregory McFordingham. I'm afraid his conscience has been neglected."

"And he has left these parts in the belief that you lie mangled and dead in that abyss," I added.

"I shall be happy to disappoint him at the proper time."

We drank the rest of the milk, and lunched from our provision baskets; but Larry was too much exhausted by the strain upon his nerves to walk amid the wild scenery of the Vöringfos, and we kept still the rest of the day. We slept at the shanty that night, and the next morning renewed our rambles. We were careful not to go very near the edges of any precipices. In the afternoon we returned to Vik. The tall man had not been there, and we concluded that he and Miles had returned to Bergen by some other route.

CHAPTER XXII.

IN WHICH PHIL AND LARRY GO THROUGH SWEDEN IN THE BLANCHE.

WE remained at Vik several days, fishing and rambling among the wild scenery, till we had fully recovered from the shock of the events at the falls. We were in the most vigorous health and spirits, and were well prepared for the long tramp before us. We had no knowledge of the future intentions of Miles Grimsby. He and his tall bravo had gone to Ulvik; but we could not learn in what direction they had gone from this place.

"I suppose it makes no difference to us where they have gone," said Larry, as we were discussing the question.

"No. Miles is satisfied that he has done his work, and believes that you will not again cross his path," I replied.

"But he will not dare to show himself at Grimsby Hall, lest Sir Philip should ask him some hard questions."

"If he does, your grandfather will be able to give him better information than he possesses, after your letter has reached its destination."

"I only hope that Miles will remain in blissful ignorance of the failure of his villany till we finish our tramps on the continent."

"Probably he will. His guilty conscience — if he is blessed with such a commodity as a conscience — will drive him into retirement for a time, until he can ascertain the result of his crime, and whether or not he will be held responsible for it. Undoubtedly he will send McFordingham to some remote part of the world, where he may not rise up against his employer."

"I think we shall not be troubled any more at present."

As I have said before, we heard nothing more of the conspirators in Norway. Early on one Monday morning we set out from Vik on our way to the Rjukanfos. Day after day we walked through the wildest scenery, or sailed on the inland lakes and rivers, enjoying every moment of the time, for we did not weary ourselves with hard walking, though we had become so toughened to the tramp, that we could easily accomplish thirty miles a day. But we were a week in reaching our destination. The Rjukanfos is a waterfall, estimated to be about nine hundred feet high. The whole region is filled with cataracts, with wild mountain gorges, and tremendous precipices. We saw what was to be seen there, and then continued on our way to Christiania, where we arrived in another week.

At the hotel in this city we found letters awaiting us, which had been forwarded by the London banker, according to our direction. Among them was one from Mr. Spelter, dated at Frederiksværn, where he had been at anchor for ten days. He informed us that the Hermia had followed him out of the Fjord from Bergen, but he had run away from her the first day out, in a fresh breeze from the westward, and he had not seen or heard anything of her since. Larry had a letter from Sir Philip, and two from Blanche Fennimore. I found several from my father and mother, and one from Ella Gracewood. The latter contained a photograph, which represented a lady so mature that I had some difficulty in believing that she was the identical little girl whom I had met on the Upper Missouri, and whom I had rescued from the Indians. I opened this letter first; but I only read enough of it to assure myself that she was well, before I attended to those from my father and mother.

I wish I could give to my readers who have not been far away from home, some idea of the dread, the excitement, and the pleasure created by the reception of letters from the loved ones on another continent. The wanderer hardly dares to open them, lest they should contain intelligence of the sickness or death of some dear one, thousands of miles away, where it is impossible to reach him without crossing the dreary waste of ocean. Relieved of this dread, the letters are then like the dews of evening to the parched earth. My father's first letter contained bad news. My grandfather, Mr. Collingsby of Chicago, had died suddenly of paralysis. My mother's letters enlarged upon the sad event, and I shed tears for her in her grief, which my own relation to the deceased could not have called forth. When I had read all the letters of my parents, I turned again to that of Ella. It was rather more reserved than I liked in its tone; but, though I was tenderly attached to her, our relations at home had been merely friendly; for I had not thought it quite right to win any promise from her until she was old enough to know her own mind. But the principal point of the letter was the announcement that, as her mother's health was again failing her, the family would sail for Europe in August, and spend the next winter in Italy. They intended to pass the months of September and October in Switzerland; and I was cheered with the hope that I might meet Ella there in our grand tramp to the south. Larry's letters were all satisfactory, and Sir Philip was still in excellent health.

We made several short trips to the interior from Christiania, and then went by steamer to Frederiksværn, where we were received on board the Blanche with cheers by the crew, for the men were tired of waiting in so dull a place. They were delighted to see us, and their faces were all decked with smiles.

"Well, how goes it, Mr. Spelter?" I asked.

"It goes heavy here, with nothing to do, and no one to help us," replied the mate. "I had to scrub the ballast, to keep the men from getting up a mutiny."

"What's the matter with them?"

"Nothing, except they want something to do. I allowed them to go on shore, and to sleep twelve hours a day. The hardest work in the world is to do nothing."

"That's true; and we will not persecute them any longer. Get under way at once."

"All hands, up anchor!" shouted the mate. "Clear away the mainsail!"

The sailors sprang to their stations with a will, and looked as cheerful as though every one of them had just inherited a fortune. In a few moments the Blanche was standing out of the harbor under all sail, for we did not even wait for a pilot. Larry and I went below as soon as the yacht was clear of the harbor.

"We don't find anything equal to this anywhere — do we, Phil?" said my friend, as he threw himself on the divan.

"Certainly not. But if we had not been on shore for three weeks, sleeping in the homely post-houses, and feeding on the simplest fare, we should not now enjoy it half so much. Our tramps make the yacht pleasanter."

"You are a philosopher, Phil, and I dare say you are right. I am sure this cabin never looked so much like a place to me as it does at this moment. I am afraid I shall not wish to leave these quarters again in a hurry."

"Well, there is no law to compel you to do so."

"But I wish to see the interior of Sweden."

"Very good; you may even do that without leaving the yacht. You can go through the Göta Canal to Stockholm."

"That's an idea, Phil."

"You may then sail all over the great lakes of Sweden," I added, taking our large atlas, and opening at the map of Norway and Sweden. "Here is Wenern Lake, one hundred miles long by fifty wide."

"I like that, Phil. The idea of sailing in the Blanche on a fresh-water lake is rather pleasant, and altogether novel."

"But you may go through three or four other lakes — Wettern, Roxen, Malar, and some smaller ones."

"Let us do it. But, Phil, how are we to beat against the wind in a canal? I don't believe the foreto'-bobbin will do that for you."

"We must have a small steamer to tow us. It will cost money; and the canal dues will be an item, also."

"Right. I am struggling with all my might to spend my income; and this trip will help me out considerably."

I was quite as well pleased with the idea as Larry was; and we sat down to dinner, still discussing the plan. I could not help contrasting our elegant dinner with the coarse meals of which we had partaken at the post-houses, for the steward seemed to have taken particular pains on the present occasion, perhaps because he had been idle so long. Life in the cabin of the Blanche was so very delightful that neither of us cared to leave it again at present.

With the fresh breeze we reached Gottenburg the next morning, and on the following day all our arrangements were completed for the trip. We engaged an interpreter to do our talking for us, though we had a Swedish sailor forward. We chartered a little steamer to tow us through, and early in the morning we sailed for our inland trip. The first part of it was through the Göta River, though we occasionally passed through a canal to avoid a rapid. In the afternoon we walked around the Falls of Trollhätten, enjoying the delightful scenery, while the Blanche was going through the long series of locks. Indeed, we had walked half the distance during the day, and Larry insisted that we were working our passage. In the evening we reached the great lake, and moored to the shore for the night.

At daylight in the morning, with a pilot on board, we sailed again, the steamer towing us out into the lake. As the sun rose, a smart breeze from the westward sprang up, and I told Mr. Spelter to hoist the mainsail and set the jib. As soon as this was done, the tow-line slackened up, and we were in great danger of running over the steamer.

"Cast off that tow-line," said I to the mate, "then set the foresail."

"Ay, ay, sir," laughed Spelter.

The order was obeyed, and the tow-boat sheered off. The foresail was hoisted, and the Blanche lay down to her work in earnest. It was soon evident that we were running away from our escort. We were bound to Carlstad, at the northern extremity of the lake. The skipper commenced a famous yelling when we began to get away from him.

"What is the matter with him?" I asked of the interpreter.

"He wants the money for towing you up from Gottenburg."

"Does he think we are going to run away from him?" laughed Larry. "Heave to on your foreto'-bobbin, Phil, and tell him I will pay him for his time till we get to Stockholm."

We came up into the wind, and allowed the steamer to approach. The interpreter explained our plan to the captain; but he was not satisfied. He insisted upon his money for what he had done, and I paid him. He promised to be at the entrance of the canal on the east shore of the lake, the next day, to tow us through. We filled away again, and the wind increased in force till we had all we could stand without shortening sail. It was not a gale; but the surface of the lake was covered with white caps, and had quite a stormy appearance. As we went out farther from the shore, we found an ugly chop sea, which kept the yacht bobbing and bowing like a French dancing-master. At breakfast time the dishes would not stay on the table.

"How's this, Phil?" said Larry, as the contents of his coffee-cup were jerked into his lap.

"Rather rough."

"Rough on my trousers, and rather warm, too," laughed he. "Why, it's worse than a gale on the ocean."

"It is one of these fresh-water seas — just what we used to have on Lake Michigan; but this yacht is so much bigger than the Ella, in which I used to sail, that it is smooth here compared with what I have seen."

"I don't like it," protested Larry.

"You will soon get used to it. Take another cup of coffee, and drink it while you may."

"No more, thank you."

"What's the matter, Larry?"

"I don't know; but I don't feel just right."

I saw that he was very pale. I may as well hasten to the sad conclusion. My friend was sea-sick. He went on deck, but was soon obliged to take to his berth. There he lay till two o'clock in the afternoon, when we made Carlstad, having logged twelve knots all day. As soon as the motion ceased, Larry immediately recovered, and ate a hearty dinner with me in the cabin. Not less than four of our seamen were sick also, the motion of the vessel on the lake was so different from that on the ocean.

"I have had enough of this thing," said Larry.

"You won't be sick again. Don't give it up so."

"I am ashamed of myself, Phil. I have crossed the Atlantic three times without being seasick; and here I am knocked over on a little fresh-water pond! It is mortifying; and I am disgusted with myself."

"It is not your fault."

"But I lose confidence in my stomach. I thought it was lined with zinc, and would stand anything. Now it has gone back on me."

"Four of our old salts were seasick, too — had to go below and turn in; men who have been to sea all their lives."

"Is that so?"

"It's a fact."

"Then I am comforted; for I am only human, like them. I like that paddling through the canal. It is the most delicious sort of idleness I ever experienced. You keep moving, and can see the people and the country as you go along. It isn't like being snaked through a country in a railroad train so fast that the telegraph poles look like a fine-tooth comb."

"If we have a breeze to-morrow, we shall be in the canal again to-morrow afternoon."

"You marine gentlemen always whistle for a breeze; and sometimes you overdo it. Don't whistle any more, Phil; and I shall be content to wait till day after to-morrow for more of the canal glories."

"I won't whistle, Larry."

We went ashore and strolled through the town. At night the lake was calm, and the next day we had only a gentle breeze. The balloon-jib was in order then, and we had a delightful passage to the canal. The pilot was astonished at the sailing qualities of the Blanche. We passed near a multitude of islands, full of natural beauty, and at noon were in the canal, where the little steamer was waiting for us. We went on till dark, and then lay up for the night, for we were unwilling to lose the view of the pleasant scenery. In this manner we passed through the canal, emerging first into a broad bay, bordered by lovely shores, and then into Lake Wettern, where we again cast off the tow-line, and for a joke towed the steamer some twenty miles to Motala, where we spent another night. Passing through another bay, another lake, and a considerable length of canal, we entered the Baltic. Coasting among the islands for a few hours, we again passed through a canal to the Malar Lake, and in the evening reached Stockholm. The trip through the canal was delightful in every respect.

We went to the Hotel Rydberg, to see who was there from our country. Larry found an English gentleman whom he had met at Grimsby Hall. While they were discussing a question which was interesting to them, but not to me, I walked out into the street to see the passers-by. The first person that attracted my attention was a gentleman six feet and a half high, with red hair. He was elegantly dressed in black; but I promptly recognized in him our old acquaintance, Captain McFordingham.

CHAPTER XXIII.

IN WHICH PHIL AND LARRY MEET McFORDINGHAM
ON TWO SPECIAL OCCASIONS.

I WAS not very much astonished to see McFordingham in Sweden, for we had last met him in Norway. A wonderful change had taken place in his appearance, for he had entirely discarded all his peculiarities of dress. He looked like a gentleman, and I am obliged to acknowledge that his air was rather "distinguished." The captain sauntered into the *café* connected with the hotel. I had no difficulty in coming to the conclusion that Miles Grimsby had paid him liberally for the foul service rendered. Through an open window I saw the captain seat himself with his back to the door. I entered, and took a place in a corner behind him, where I could look out into the street.

As the satellite was here, I supposed that Miles could not be far off, and it was probable that the

Hermia was also in port. I sat for half an hour watching the movements of the tall villain. He sipped his brandy in silence; but Miles did not join him. I went to the porter's office, and examined the list of guests in the house; but I found neither the name of the master nor the man. On my return to the *café*, McFordingham was conversing with an English gentleman who was seated opposite to him. I placed myself near enough to hear them; but, as they were talking in quite a loud tone, this was no breach of propriety. I noticed that the stranger called the captain Major Lord. I had seen this name on the porter's book. The convict had found it best to change his name. Something was said about the ladies, and a ride to the Deer Garden, which is the principal park of the city. Presently the two gentlemen rose, and I put my face behind a newspaper, to avoid being recognized.

In a few moments more a carriage was drawn up in front of the hotel. The English gentleman and two ladies appeared, attended by McFordingham, who very politely handed them to their seats. The ladies were both elegant in their manners, and one of them was quite pretty.

"Who are they?" I asked, when the porter returned to the hall.

"One of the gentlemen is Sir Walbridge Blount, and the other Major Lord. One of the ladies is Sir Walbridge's wife, and I really don't know who the other is," answered the porter. "They are going out to the Deer Garden, and will dine at Hasselbacken."

"What's up, Phil?" asked Larry, coming down from the room of his friend at this moment.

"Our excellent friend, Captain McFordingham, is here," I replied.

"And Miles?" he asked, with a start.

"I haven't seen him." And I stated the circumstances under which I had observed the convict. "We will dine at Hasselbacken, Larry, if you please."

"Certainly, Phil, if such is your pleasure."

"I will not allow this villain to impose himself upon respectable people," I protested. "Doubtless he thrust himself upon them, as he did upon us, on the train or the steamer. He is a plausible fellow, and I suppose Sir Walbridge has not an army list with him."

We drove to the Deer Garden, and in the

course of the afternoon, after we had examined the beauties of the place, we found Sir Walbridge's party in a pavilion, waiting for dinner. We took places near them, but behind the captain. He was very attentive to the fairer of the two ladies, who sat opposite him. After the soup, he rose to pick up her handkerchief, which she had dropped. As he was returing to his place, he happened to glance at me. He started and turned pale, but he did not see Larry, whose back was to him.

"Ah, Captain McFordingham!" I exclaimed, loud enough for all the party to hear me.

As I spoke, I rose and advanced towards him. He was very pale, but he did not lose his self-possession, or, rather, his impudence.

"This is very unexpected, Captain McFordingham," I added, laying particular stress on the name.

"Major Lord, if you please," said he, coolly, adjusting an eye-glass over his left eye, and gazing at me with a sort of pitying and contemptuous expression. "I believe I have not the pleasure of your acquaintance. May I beg the favor of your name?"

"You knew my name well enough when you

were a convict at the Bermudas," I replied, so distinctly that all the party could understand me.

"I have not the least recollection of ever having seen you before," he added, adjusting his glass again. "You have mistaken the person; and any such indecent allusion as you made to me just now will subject you to personal chastisement."

"Nevertheless, you are what I say you are — a convict, transported for embezzling your master's property."

"The presence of these ladies insures your personal safety for the present; but we shall meet again, if you don't run away," said he.

"Or you don't," I added.

He seated himself again, and resumed his polite attentions to the lady in front of him, who seemed to be very much embarrassed by the scene which had just transpired.

"Ah, Mr. Grimsby, I am glad to meet you again," said a young gentleman, stepping up to our table at this moment. "You said you would not come to Hasselbacken with me."

"I didn't know that I would then. I told you I must join my friend, Captain Farringford, whom permit me to introduce."

It was Mr. Whistleton, whose acquaintance Larry had made at Grimsby Hall. I shook hands with him, and he joined us at dinner.

"Ah, Whistleton, are you here?" said Sir Walbridge.

"I am here. This is Mr. Lawrence Grimsby, of Grimsby Hall, and this is Captain Farringford," replied our new friend. "And this is Major Lord, formerly of the India service."

Larry rose and bowed as his name was mentioned. Major Lord sprang to his feet, and shook like an aspen, as he gazed at the form and features of his late victim.

"You have seen him before, if you haven't seen me," I suggested.

"Excuse me, ladies; I thought it was Mr. Miles Grimsby, who assured me a week ago that he was on his way to Italy, and I was utterly astounded to meet him here."

"This is a very pretty farce, Captain McFordingham," added Larry.

"You insist that I shall be Captain McFordingham, in spite of my protest, and I may as well submit," said the tall villain, with a sickly smile.

"I shall insist," replied Larry. "If you don't

believe that you are Captain McFordingham, I have the means at hand of proving it to your entire satisfaction, and that of your friends."

"Clearly a mistake," added the captain. "Perhaps I may accept your apology, when you are ready to offer it."

He seated himself again, and Sir Walbridge's party seemed to be too much confounded to say anything more; but I observed a marked coldness on the part of the ladies towards him. Mr. Whistleton informed us that the lady upon whom the captain lavished his attentions was Sir Walbridge's wife's sister, and that she had a fortune in her own right. In the evening we returned to the city.

Of course Sir Walbridge and the ladies were very much disturbed by the events of the afternoon, and were anxious to obtain an explanation. But McFordingham was always in the way. I invited Mr. Whistleton to visit the yacht, which was now moored at the quay near the palace. We slept on board, as usual.

Early the next morning, Mr. Whistleton, attended by Sir Walbridge, came on board, and we gave them a full history of McFordingham. They had made his acquaintance in Copenhagen, and he had accompanied them through the Göta Canal. I assured them that every one of my crew could identify him, and referred them also to Lady Eleanor and Mr. Langford in England. They were satisfied, and we went up to the hotel with them. McFordingham was in the coffee-room, apparently waiting for them.

"I am satisfied now that you are an impostor and a villain," Sir Walbridge began, warmly. "If you presume to speak again to either of the ladies whose acquaintance you made under a fictitious name, I will horsewhip you at the first convenient opportunity."

"Sir Walbridge, I am the victim of false representations," protested McFordingham.

"I don't wish to hear another lie from your lips. I have investigated the subject for myself. I have nothing more to say."

Sir Walbridge and Mr. Whistleton left the *café*

"I am indebted to *you* for this," said the villain, walking sharply up to me.

"You are," I replied. "I deemed it my duty to expose an impostor."

"We need not quarrel," he added, biting his lips.

"No; but we must agree to disagree."

"I bear no malice. Miles Grimsby has gone to Italy. We have separated."

"It was time you did so. I suppose you have been well paid for your services."

"My fortune is made; and I shall be as glad to serve you as I was to serve Miles."

"We do not need your aid."

"Well, then, if you will tell me which way you are going, I will go the other way. I can injure you, but I have no desire to do so. We will be quits, if you say so."

"We shall be quits, any way, until you attempt to impose upon respectable people. Then I will go a thousand miles to expose you," I added.

"As you please. I am rather surprised to see Mr. Grimsby here," said he, coolly, as he glanced at my friend. "Certainly he fell over that precipice."

"Certainly I did, Captain McFordingham," interposed Larry; "but, being used to hard knocks, my fall did not seriously injure me, as you perceive."

"You seem to be sound."

"Quite so; no thanks to you."

"But I did the best I could to save you; and, failing of you, to save your friend. But I suppose my efforts startled you, and caused you to fall."

"Very likely. I suppose Miles went over in the same way. I think you said he had gone to Italy."

"That was an amiable fiction, merely intended to distract the attention of Captain Farringford, who was disposed to discharge his pistol at me. Miles has gone to Italy, and believes that his cousin is dead. He is satisfied, and so am I; though it appears that you were not injured by your fall. I am glad you were not. I should have been unhappy all my days in the thought that you had lost your life through my injudicious attempt to save you. It is well as it is. Let us part in peace. Good morning, gentlemen."

He turned on his heel, and abruptly left us, bowing himself out with his usual politeness.

We saw the sights of Stockholm and its vicinity with Sir Walbridge's party, and then invited them to go to St. Petersburg with us in the Blanche. They accepted the invitation. We went to Moscow and Nijni, and then returned to the capital. With our friends still on board, we cruised in the Baltic to Copenhagen, where our guests left us.

We went round to Hamburg, and directed Mr. Spelter to sail the Blanche to Genoa. Larry and I started upon another tramp across the country. But we intended to walk only through the most interesting regions; and we went by railway to Cologne. From this point we tramped on the banks of the Rhine to Baden-Baden. We travelled slowly, and enjoyed ourselves all the time.

At Baden-Baden we found McFordingham again, staking large sums at the gambling tables, with what success we had no means of knowing. He appeared to be on excellent terms with some of the "first families," and to be in the enjoyment of the smiles of the ladies. We asked his name, and ascertained that he was now "Major McPherson, formerly of the India service." I wondered that he was not a colonel by this time, since his promotions were in his own hands. But he seemed to cling to the rank of major. Larry and I walked up to the table where he was an interested actor in the game of *rouge-et-noir*.

"What luck do you have, Captain McFordingham?" said Larry, in a tone loud enough to startle all near the table, where silence is the prevailing rule.

The tall man suddenly turned upon my friend as though he had been electrified by a bolt from the clouds. His wrath overcame his coolness and his politeness this time, and he sprang at Larry's throat with the fierceness of a bloodhound. This conduct was so utterly different from anything he had exhibited before that I was startled by it; but I promptly rushed to the assistance of my companion. With the help of others, I dragged the villain off, and a policeman interfered after the scuffle was over.

"You are violent, Captain McFordingham," said Larry, restoring his deranged dress.

"There is some mistake," interposed an English gentleman. "This is Major McPherson."

"Not at all. He is not even a captain in any service, but was the footman of Lord Bergamot, and was sentenced to ten years' transportation for embezzling his master's property."

"Lord Bergamot's footman!" exclaimed the Englishman. "Impossible!"

"Quite impossible," added McFordingham, who had by this time recovered his temper and his self-possession. "This American person, with whom I had some difficulty in Stockholm, takes the most

dishonorable method of annoying me. I regret that I allowed my temper to get the better of me; but I purpose to chastise this individual at a proper time."

"You have attempted to chastise him several times before," said Larry.

"Did I hear my name mentioned here?" said a gentleman of thirty years of age on the outskirts of the crowd, who had evidently just entered the room.

"That depends upon what your name is, sir," I suggested.

"I am Lord Bergamot, and I thought I heard my name as I came in."

"You did, sir. Do you happen to know that tall gentleman?" I asked, pointing to the captain, whom he had not yet seen.

"'Pon my word!" exclaimed his lordship, pushing his way into the centre of the group. "Why, Greg, are you here? and dressed like a gentleman, too?"

"Lord Bergamot!" ejaculated the English gentleman who had taken a prominent part in the scene; "some one here says Major McPherson was your footman."

"Pray, who is Major McPherson?" asked his lordship, as the convict tried to slink away.

"Why, the tall gentleman."

"That was my man Greg, surely. I have really forgotten his other name."

"McFordingham," I added.

"That's it. He is no major; and, I am sorry to say, he was sent to the Bermudas for ten years for stealing my plate and other valuables. — Isn't that so, Greg?"

But Greg had crept out of the room, and Larry and I had a chance to tell our story. The rascal left the place at once, and that was the last we ever saw of him, though we heard of him again, when, after he had spent all his ill-gotten wealth, he was transported to Botany Bay for picking a gentleman's pocket.

CHAPTER XXIV.

IN WHICH PHIL AND LARRY FINISH THEIR TRAMPS, AND SETTLE DOWN FOR LIFE.

LEAVING Baden-Baden, we walked through the Black Forest to Schaffhausen; and, after a day at the Falls of the Rhine, we continued the tramp to Zurich, where, to my great joy, I found the Gracewoods. My old instructor gave me a cordial greeting, and said I had grown so much, and looked so brown and tough, he should hardly have known me. Ella received me with a blush, and with a degree of emotion which assured me that I had not been long out of her mind at any time, as she had not been out of mine. It took a whole day to discuss the past, and we reviewed all the events which had occurred in the wilds of the Upper Missouri.

In memory of old times we took a boat, and I rowed her far out upon the lake. She had grown tall and graceful in form, and had really become a woman. As I sat in the boat facing her, gently plying the oars, we spoke of the days when I had so often rowed her upon the Missouri. From this I was led to tell her how much I thought of her then; and, of course, I could not help adding that my views had not changed, and, more than this, they never would change. Indeed, I believe I said a great many things that would seem very silly to anybody else, and therefore I shall not repeat them. "I had carried her image in my heart in all my wanderings," and all that sort of thing. Had she ever thought of me? And she answered me in monosyllables, at first, till finally we came to an excellent understanding in regard to the matter which was nearest to the hearts of both of us.

Somehow I felt very ethereal when I landed, and walked by Ella's side to the hotel. Everything looked airy to me, and I felt perfectly satisfied with myself and everybody else, especially the fair girl at my side. I don't know whether we made any promises or not. It did not seem to me that any were necessary, for when she pressed my hand in response to the pressure of my own, it was to me the significant telegraphy of hearts that required no formal interpretation in cold words. That evening I spoke to her father on the subject, who only laughed, and said he and Mrs. Gracewood had long regarded it as a foregone conclusion.

We staid a week at Zurich, which, somehow, I have ever since regarded as the pleasantest place in all Switzerland, and that lake like the streams of Paradise; but doubtless the opinion was the result of association, and I am not disposed to quarrel with those who think Lucerne is a more agreeable residence.

Larry was in a hurry to resume our tramps, and to join the yacht at Genoa; but he bore with me patiently for several days, under the circumstances. The doctors had advised Mrs. Gracewood to try the climate of Sicily in November, and I expected the Blanche would put into Messina on her return from the Upper Mediterranean, so that I was comforted with the hope of meeting Ella again in two months.

Larry and I walked to Lucerne, and, passing through the lake by steamer, set out upon our tramp over the Pass of St. Gothard. We spent a week on the road, and another on the Italian lakes, so that it was the middle of September when we reached Genoa. The Blanche had been in port a fortnight, and Mr. Spelter, to keep the men contented, had thoroughly overhauled the vessel, and given her a fresh coat of paint, so that she presented a very neat appearance when we went on board. We spent a couple of days in Genoa, and then sailed for Naples.

"What yacht is that, Mr. Spelter?" I asked, as the Blanche approached the Mole.

"If I'm not mistaken, it is the Hermia," replied the mate.

"McFordingham said Miles had gone to Italy; but I did not suppose he spoke the truth," I added.

We anchored near her, and we had hardly secured our sails before a boat put off from her and came alongside the Blanche. Osborne was in the stern-sheets. I did not suppose that he knew anything about the events which had transpired in Norway, for Miles had probably been careful to keep his terrible secret in his own bosom; but I concluded that he had sent his sailing-master to see me, and hear what I had to say. Osborne asked me where we had been cruising, and similar questions. He did not seem to be at all astonished at seeing Larry, and I was sure that the secret had not been imparted to him.

"Is Mr. Grimsby on board?" I asked.

"No, sir. He is sick on shore," replied Osborne. "We have been waiting three weeks for him."

"What ails him?"

"Well, I don't know exactly what it is; but it's a malignant fever — contagious, too."

"When did you see him last?"

"I haven't seen him since he went on shore."

"Is he very sick?"

"I believe he is. There is a great deal of sickness here. Typhoid fever, I think it is."

"But haven't you seen him?" asked Larry.

"No. It's bad enough to stay here when there's so much sickness, without going to see anybody that has the fever," said Osborne.

"Who takes care of him?"

"I don't know. He sent down for some of the hands to stay with him; but none of them would go."

"At what hotel is he staying?"

Osborne mentioned one of the hotels where he had been at first, but believed he was not there now. He couldn't ascertain anything about him, and didn't know but he was dead. We were astonished at the heartlessness of the sailing-master, though, from what we knew of his character, we could hardly expect anything better of him. Larry and I went on shore immediately, and visited the hotel named by Osborne. Mr. Miles Grimsby had been there, but, being sick with a malignant disease, had been removed to a boarding-house. Procuring the services of a *commissionaire*, we found the place with much difficulty. It was a mean house, scantily furnished, and the patient had been conveyed to the upper story. We found that he was very sick indeed, and was not expected to recover; and Larry was shocked, and insisted upon going directly to the chamber of Miles.

"That won't do, Larry," I interposed.

"Why not? He is my cousin; and, though he has been my enemy, I will not leave him to die in such a hole as this," he replied, indignantly.

"But you forget; Miles supposes you are dead. If you go into his chamber, the shock might kill him."

"Perhaps you are right. But we must get him out of this den."

"I will see him, Larry."

"I do not ask you to expose yourself to the disease, Phil."

"I am not afraid of it."

The *commissionaire* would not go with me, so great was his dread of the malady, and an old woman, who appeared to be Miles's nurse, conducted me to his chamber. The room contained only a bed and a chair, and was filthy enough to breed a pestilence without any help from the sewers and the malaria. I should not have recognized Miles, so fearfully was he altered; and he seemed to me to be at death's door. He looked at me, and started as he identified me.

"Farringford!" gasped he, and covered his face with the dirty bed-clothes.

"You are very sick, Miles," I said, in the gentlest tones.

"You have come to curse me," he groaned.

"No; I have come to save you."

"Nothing can save me now. I'm going to die, and everybody has deserted me. My cousin haunts me day and night." And he groaned in his misery.

"Be calm, Miles, and we will try to do something for you."

"You can't do anything for me," he answered, throwing down the bed-clothes from his face. "O, Farringford, I am cursed of God and man!"

"O, no. Be calm."

"I can't be calm. I have destroyed my cousin. I thought it would make me happy. It has made me miserable. It will kill me. Can I be forgiven before I die?"

"If you are truly penitent, you can."

"But Lawrence is dead, and I — "

He wept like a little child, in his remorse and agony.

"He is not dead," I replied, gently.

"Not dead?" he gasped, starting up in bed.

"No, not dead. He is alive and well, and at this moment trying to serve you."

"You are cheating me, Farringford," he added, fixing the gaze of his hollow eyes upon me with intense earnestness.

"I am not. You shall see him to-day."

"But I paid McFordingham five thousand pounds for what he told me he had done."

"McFordingham believed that he had pushed

Larry over the precipice; but the rope saved him," I replied, explaining the matter very briefly.

"But I am just as guilty as though I had murdered him," he continued, musing, with a vacant expression.

"I think you are."

"Will he forgive me? Will he let me die in peace?"

"He will be glad to forgive you."

"Let me see him. Let me beg his forgiveness on my knees."

He tried to get out of the bed, but the old woman restrained him. I never saw a man in such agony of mind. Deserted by every friend, and left to die in this comfortless apartment, how poor and mean his past life seemed to him! How utterly worthless the title and the fortune of his grandfather were, compared with that peace of mind which now, at the portal of the tomb, was lost to him! Even Miles was conquered, and saw at last that earth had nothing for which a man could safely barter his eternal hope.

I went down and called Larry, who followed me up to the chamber. Miles shrank and trembled as he entered. My friend took his hand, and spoke gently to him.

"Can you forgive me, Lawrence?" groaned the sufferer.

"With all my heart," replied Larry, pressing his hand. "It makes me as happy as it does you to do so. May God forgive you, too; and he will forgive you if you truly repent."

"I have cried out in misery and remorse for weeks in this bed," whispered Miles, exhausted by his emotions. "If I could only die in peace!"

Larry said all he could to comfort him. We read the Bible and prayed with him, and he was calmer. My friend had sent the *commissionaire* for a celebrated English physician who resided in the city, when he learned that no proper medical man had attended him. The doctor came, but thought the patient's case was almost hopeless. His only chance was in a removal from the pestilential locality in which his present lodging was situated. It was but a short distance from the Mole, and was infected by the sewers. Larry paid, without a murmur, the exorbitant demands of the people in the house. I procured one of the covered hand-barrows used to carry the sick or wounded to the hospitals, and attended by Dr. Bishop, we conveyed Miles on board the Blanche. He was placed in the broad berth of Larry's room.

"Now, hoist your sails, and go to Messina," said the doctor, after he had prescribed for his patient.

We were glad enough to obey this order, and to escape the sewers of Naples, which are the bane of the city. Osborne was ordered to sail the Hermia to England.

We had a smooth sea and a light breeze, so that the voyage was not uncomfortable to the sick man. Larry nursed his cousin day and night with the most assiduous care. We had a long passage to Messina; but on our arrival the health officers drove us into quarantine. As there was no sickness there, we did not object. Miles had already begun to improve in the change of air and with the careful nursing we gave him. But I think that his peace of mind did quite as much as the nursing and the change to save him. He declared that he was ready to die now; but this submission only contributed to his recovery. In a week he was able to sit up. We gave him the nourishing food and cordials which the doctor had prescribed, with wonderful effect. In another week he went on deck, and we sailed for Constantinople. As we moved gently along among the fair islands of the

Archipelago, he lay on the deck, wrapped up in his robes. Larry read the Bible and other good books to him, and watched over him with a woman's tenderness.

As I sat near my friend one day, while we were going through the Sea of Marmora, listening to his reading, Miles suddenly burst into tears. I was not greatly surprised at this demonstration, for he had often exhibited evidences of tenderness since he came on board the yacht which had before seemed utterly foreign to his nature. He had been at death's door, and in this condition was deserted by his friends, or, rather, by his dependants. He had given himself up to die alone, and in the midst of those who cared only to get his last dollar when the breath had left his body. To be saved from such a fate, and be nursed tenderly by the kindest of friends, was more than he could bear. It overcame him; it broke down his worldly pride.

"What are you, Lawrence?" he asked, wiping the tears from his thin, pale face.

"Yours, truly," replied Larry, lightly.

"I think you are an angel. I can't help saying so when I think of the past."

"O, nonsense!"

"I have pursued you like a fiend; I have paid thousands of pounds to destroy you; I have hated you with all the intensity of my nature; and yet you are willing to risk your life, to expose yourself to a malignant disease, to save me. Why have you done so?"

"I'll tell you, Miles. When you shut me up in my state-room for two days on board of the Whitewing, I found the Bible in my room. I suppose you did not know it was there."

"I did not know there was one on board of the yacht."

"There was one in that state-room, and I read it for two days. If there had been no Bible there, I might have shot you on the cliff at Cherrystone Hill; I might have tumbled you over the precipice at the Vöringfos — I don't know. If Christ could forgive those who crucified him, surely we ought to try to forgive those who seek to injure us in this world. I don't boast of myself. I only try to do my duty. It is hard work sometimes, and we can only succeed with the help of God."

"I am trying with you now, Lawrence."

"I know you are; and we will cling to each

other, while we cling together to the religion of Jesus Christ. Sir Philip will be glad to see us now."

"May he be long spared to us!"

"As to that title, Miles —"

"It is yours; and, though I become a beggar, I shall now be more rejoiced to see you have it than to have it myself," said Miles, warmly, and sincerely, I fully believe, for he had already begun to "read his title clear to mansions in the skies;" and this earthly distinction looked vain and empty.

"I have always begged Sir Philip to treat us both alike. I am sure that he will do so now," added Larry.

Miles was conquered, overcome, by the power of love and faith. Larry's triumph was complete, and he had attained the end for which he labored and prayed. We arrived at Constantinople that evening. We saw all its strange sights, and we explored the Bosphorus and the Black Sea. We went to the Holy Land next; and in the midst of the scenes where Christ had lived and died, our faith was rekindled and renewed. Miles was by this time able to travel on shore, and his impressions and emotions were even stronger than Larry's.

He was a changed man, and far more demonstrative in his religious observances than his cousin. He was now as zealous in the right as he had been before in the wrong.

In November, after a tour up the Nile, we sailed for Messina. We found the Gracewoods there, and I had no longer any occasion to complain of the reserve of Ella. The delicious climate had already produced a favorable effect upon Mrs. Gracewood's health. With the family on board the Blanche, we made an excursion to Malta and Palermo. Indeed, we spent the winter in cruising about the shores of the Mediterranean. We visited all the Italian and Spanish ports, and in April, with the Gracewoods on board, we sailed from Lisbon for Cowes. On our arrival we hastened to Grimsby Hall, where Sir Philip clasped both his grandsons in one embrace.

Miles had sent his yacht home, and directed his agent to discharge her crew, and sell her, for he was utterly disgusted with Osborne and the rest of his people. Larry declared that one yacht was quite enough for both of them.

In May, with the Gracewoods still on board, we sailed for New York, where we arrived after a rather long passage, though to me it was the pleasantest I ever made, for Ella was on board.

Of course Larry hastened to Blanche Fennimore as soon as the anchor touched the ground. He had been absent over a year, and I doubt not the warmth of his welcome was in proportion to the length of his absence. Leaving him in the most exuberant happiness, I went to St. Louis with the Gracewoods. I need not attempt to tell how glad my father and mother were to see me. I was at home again.

My father was still true to himself, and he was more respected than he had been in his former prosperity, for all his business transactions were gauged by religious principle now. He stood high in the church and high in the exchange, for no one accused him of hypocrisy. My grandfather's estate had been settled, and my mother's property, which she unreservedly confided to her husband's keeping, made him rich again. He was now the owner of several steamboats; and my old friend, Captain Davis, is in command of the Gracewood. Our home is as happy as my brightest dream ever pictured it.

For two years I went as clerk of the Gracewood, and often revisited the scenes of my early life on the Upper Missouri; but now the march of civilization is stealing over it, and the face of the country is entirely changed. A large village has grown up at the mouth of the creek where the wood-yard was, and wheat-fields wave where the " Castle " stood.

My father built a new steamer, which he called the Ella, and, after an experience of two years as a clerk, the command of her was given to me. But I was soon in command of another Ella, or, rather, she was in command of me, for she always had her own way. Our bridal tour was a trip to Europe, a month of which we spent at Grimsby Hall with Mr. and Mrs. Lawrence Grimsby. Sir Philip still held on to his title, which Miles no longer coveted. He was a hale, hearty old man, and was eighty-two before I was called upon to address my friend as Sir Lawrence Grimsby.

I found that Miles was as busy as a bee all the time, as the patron of scores of religious and charitable movements. He was an earnest and sincere Christian, and had no occupation but to do good to the poor, the ignorant, and the vicious.

After a six months' tour in Europe we returned

to America, and settled down in St. Louis. Our firm is FARRINGFORD & SON, for my father was no more disposed to retire from business than I was. My wife never makes any ill-natured allusions to mothers-in-law, though both members of the firm live under one roof. My father and mother are quite as happy as Ella and myself, and their greatest pride and joy are in their grandchildren. It is years since I have seen Sir Lawrence, for the little ones have kept both of us at home. He does not keep a yacht. He sold the Blanche when he was married, and went with his bride to reside at Grimsby Hall. But my friend writes to me occasionally, and always has a great deal to say about Miles. He counts it as one of the happiest events of our ONWARD AND UPWARD life that his cousin was "born again," as the chief incident of that eventful year on SEA AND SHORE.

www.ingramcontent.com/pod-product-compliance
Lightning Source LLC
Chambersburg PA
CBHW032043220426
43664CB00008B/838